Celebrity Detox

rosie
o'donnell

Celebrity Detox

(the fame game)

GRAND CENTRAL
PUBLISHING

NEW YORK   BOSTON

Grand Central Publishing
Hachette Book Group USA
237 Park Avenue
New York, NY 10017

Visit our Web site at www.HachetteBookGroupUSA.com.

Printed in the United States of America

First Edition: October 2007
10 9 8 7 6 5 4 3 2 1

Grand Central Publishing is a division of Hachette Book
Group USA, Inc.
The Grand Central Publishing name and logo is a trademark
of Hachette Book Group USA, Inc.

ISBN-10: 0-446-58224-7
ISBN-13: 978-0-446-58224-7

Library of Congress Control Number: 2007929807

Book design and text composition by Ellen Rosenblatt/SDDesigns

To my mother and yours.

Thanks to:

Lauren Slater
Jamie Raab
Ed O'Donnell
Michele Riordan Read
Vivian Polak
Nan-jo

Contents

Celebrity Detox

CHAPTER 1

The Two Bs

My mother loved Barbra Streisand. A lot. She had all her records, plus she watched her whenever she did a talk show or had a TV special. My mother listened to *Funny Girl* on the blue Victrola cabinet she got at the flea market, a cabinet she stripped and stained herself somehow, alone in the garage. My mom had five kids and her own mother living with her. How did she have time to do anything? I have four kids, a wife, and two nannies, and I am often overwhelmed.

My mother took the time out to fill up on yellow. Yellow is my shorthand for *real*, for *true*, for *beauty*. Yellow means what is good with our world. My mother knew yellow. We watched Billie Jean King together as she beat Bobby Riggs. My mother took us to Radio City to see the Christmas show. My mother pointed out the women who had risen above what it meant to be a

1

woman, back then in the 1960s, and even now too. "Streisand," my mother would say, "look at her, from Brooklyn, look at her now."

"Anything is possible, little girl." My mother told me this, in her own way, usually without words. Irish people are sometimes not so good with words. They are sometimes not so good with feelings. That's why inside I'm a Jew. I want to feel it, talk it, live it, scream it. I want it all out there.

At some point in my childhood, my mother told me about Barbara Walters. Probably she pointed her out to me on the TV. This woman was a weather girl who worked her way up to being co-anchor with Harry Reasoner, who interviewed every world leader, and she did all this at a time when women were told it was impossible. She paved the way for Oprah and Katie Couric and Diane Sawyer and every TV newswoman, every female TV personality for that matter. My mother recognized Barbara Walters's meaning from the get-go.

We used to watch Barbara Walters. My mother recognized that Walters was always imparting two levels of information, the spoken and the implicit. The spoken was the this and that of the day's news. The implicit was that it was now possible for a woman to deliver that news. We watched Barbara Walters's phenomenal rise to the top. We watched, more closely still, the wide wake she left, a path I think my mother wanted me to see. Barbra Streisand, she was about the ultimate; she was genius incarnate. She was a goddess to us, while Walters was of this world. What Barbara Walters proved to us was that women could rise in this world. What Barbra Streisand proved to us was that art was beyond gender, and through it one could rise right beyond this world, and get to someplace better.

Several years ago I left my show. I'd lost the ability to get to the place Streisand had shown me was possible. Six years of celebrity-hood had left me depleted, and I had to find myself, find my art, and find my family again. I went off the air so I could touch down on the ground. And I did. And the ground felt good. I had my kids back—Chelsea, Parker, Blake, and Vivi. I had my wife. Kel and I had started up a gay cruise ship business and twice a year we went sailing with other gay families. We filmed it all and made a documentary of what it means to be a gay family. We screened the documentary one night at the New York Arts Center. This was in April 2006. One month prior to this, March 17, had been the thirty-third anniversary of my mother's death. There were rumors, sometime around then, that Streisand was thinking, at age sixty-four, of going back on tour. It was April in New York City, the trees were putting on green sleeves, boats were back on the Hudson, and my movie was finally done.

And so Barbara Walters came to this first screening. She wasn't a stranger to me. Not only had I spent much of my childhood watching her on TV and, more significant still, watching my mother watch her on TV, I'd also known her as an adult, in my own right. I'd had dinner with Barbara Walters, and she'd even been to our home to interview Kelli once. We were friends in the celebrity kind of way—you know and respect each other—you have dinner every few months. You don't chat on the phone, but there is an undeniable association, a shared intimacy that paradoxically lacks all intimacy. You are members of an exclusive club where everyone speaks a language very few others have been able to attain. Fame.

A few weeks before the premiere of my documentary, I'd been to a party at Barbara's house. This was a party for Mike Bloomberg, and Kel got all dressed up to go. Kel looked beautiful. She always does. I was wearing my standard black pants from Target and my J. Jill clogs, and we went uptown, and we were curious. We'd never seen Barbara Walters's house before. Going there was a fairly big deal. We rode the elevator up and walked into a stunning red room, and there was Barbara, in the center, wearing a beautiful gold lamé evening gown, the same one she probably wore to interview some heads of state.

Maybe Idi Amin Dada or Prince Charles or even the Da-
lai Lama. She looked flawless and stunning in her bright
red room, a Julian Schnabel painting on the wall, a double
piano, the keys as white as teeth, a man in a tux playing.
I was, well, I was enchanted, almost flabbergasted—the
color, the beauty, the women with their silk sheaths and
the hors d'oeuvres served on trays with scalloped rims.
A lot of people might assume that's what celebrities do,
go to fancy parties with double baby grands in merlot-
colored rooms, but the fact is, I don't. Mostly, especially
since leaving my show, I'm home with Kel and the kids,
eating string-bean casseroles with fried onions on top,
Blake's favorite. I remember a waiter whisked by, offer-
ing me some flaky layered thing.

At dinner I sat next to Liz Smith. I think it was
during the serving of the second course that in walked
this woman, gorgeous, I mean, she looked like Ann-
Margret meets Jessica Rabbit. She had a Clinton-like
charisma. When I asked, "Who the hell is that?" Liz
Smith said, "That's Georgette Mosbacher." Georgette
looked at me from across the room. She seemed dream-
like. I said to Barbara Walters, "I have to know her."
Barbara may not have taken me seriously at first.
"Look, Barbara," I kept saying, "I'm enchanted." I
don't know if Barbara arranged it or not, but not long
after Georgette came over to me. She leaned in real
close and said, "I'm a Republican, don't tell anyone.
I'm in the closet!"

❧

People have questioned me about the way I'm drawn to certain people, men and women both. My attractions to other people are not sexual in any sense. That seems hard for people to really believe. There was, for instance, a weekend when Jane Fonda came to visit me. We were in my craft room. I was showing her some art I had made. In one of my collages was a photograph of Madonna. "You two were lovers?" Jane Fonda said, more of a statement than a question. I said, "No, we were never ever lovers. We were sisters from the moment we met." There was never anything sexual about it. This surprised Jane. Her surprise surprised me.

❧

After dinner the night of Barbara's party, I remember singing "Liza With a 'Z'" as a beautiful old-school pianist played on the baby grand. I could *feel* Barbara Walters watching me. Sometimes that happens. A stare seems to have weight, or touch. Someone's eyes land on you. That night it was Barbara's eyes, mixed up with my voice, as I sang "Liza With a 'Z.'" I was in Barbara's world, and the song was a string pulling her back, I think, to the days when she was younger, when her father, Lou Walters, who owned the famous Latin Quarter nightclub, was alive. I believe that song brought her back to something in her past, and I could see her seeing me, Barbara Walters, the woman my mother admired for the wide wake she made, the woman who, in delivering news, became news herself.

I am drawn to many people in many different ways—sister, friend, buddy, colleague—but to Barbara, I was drawn differently. Perhaps because my mother died when I was still a child, I will forever in certain instances see women who are much older than I am as a child might. Barbara was the age my mother would have been had she survived her cancer. And I also knew Barbara had a daughter, and was therefore a mother. When I saw Barbara, I saw my mother seeing her; I saw the television in our house on Rhonda Lane, and the gray telephone poles supporting miles and miles of wires stretching high up a hill, toward a place we could never get to.

Maybe the song was bringing Barbara back to her past; all I knew was at that moment we shared something real. I wondered what it was. And then the song ended. It was time to go home. We left the red room, and during the many many months I worked on *The View* I was not invited back.

But the room left an impression on me, so much so that even now, if I close my eyes, I can see still its hue, a red that resists words but that pulses on nevertheless, a color too rich, too much, like the woman herself; she is striking and beautiful, but also blinding, Barbara

Walters, her beautiful red giving off a glare that makes one want to wince, in both pleasure and pain, and then to turn toward something softer.

⁓

Two weeks after the red room, the party, I invited Barbara Walters to the premiere of my documentary, and I'm glad I did it. I'm proud of that film. It shows gay families as they really are, struggling with all the same things every other family struggles with: sunscreen, diapers, sippy cups, and stubbornness. What makes the film so moving is how grateful the families are to finally have a place, *some* place, to go together. I'm also proud to have made it at a time when my career was down in the dumps because here I was doing something, creating a whole other thing. There was beauty and truth in that movie, a film about children and parents, about love and human equality and vulnerability. The women who directed it get all the credit. I'm not sure I could have put it together and said so succinctly what it is that gay families are about without their help. The movie ends with a view of the huge ship on the Caribbean blue waters.

And then the lights went back on and people rustled up out of their seats. I was in the lobby and I saw Barbara Walters come out of the theater, crying. "Rosie," she said, "would you ever consider being the permanent co-host of *The View*?"

I looked her in the eyes. That she was moved moved me. That she had shown working-class women like my mother that a wider wake was possible—that moved me too. I'd been out of show business for four years, a sacred silence this had been, but maybe I was ready to go back. What happened next I didn't plan. I certainly could never have anticipated it and still today I can't explain it. All I know is this. "Barbara Walters," I said. "I'll do whatever you ask."

As it turns out, I did not do whatever she asked. I came on *The View*, and this is the story of how it all happened, offstage, onstage, how we struggled to make the show, and then so much more than that. This is an account of what it means to make a show, and a friend, and an enemy, or two. This is about where we went wrong, and right. It's a story about stars and celebrities and one woman—me—going off air four years ago and then trying to reenter orbit, not knowing if she can. It's the story of wondering whether I could give up the addictive elixir of fame and then go back, wondering if it's possible to sip instead of slug. It's a revision of a book I did four years ago, just as I left my show, but trashed because it was too soon. I could go on and on, it's a story about so much, but the only thing that matters here, now, is her question, "Will you come?" and my response, "I'll do whatever you ask," and how over the year that turned out not to be true at all, how I did not do whatever Barbara Walters asked, how in fact I did very little of what she asked, how she started as a sort of mother, and me a child willing to obey, and where we finally ended up, months later, two very different women with very different values, living in very different rooms, battered by betrayal but nevertheless doing what women all over the world do best. Barbara Walters and I, after all that happened over those hard months, after all the Trump dump and divisive ways of the world we are in, we have still, and nevertheless, at the very end, we have found a way to talk. We have found, dare I say, a way to love? We found, I have to hope, a friendship that, like any other friendship, is both compromised and connected.

CHAPTER 2

Fame Is Like a Tattoo

Q&A with Lauren Slater

LAUREN: So, you've been off the air for how long now?

ROSIE: Four years?

L: And if you had to sum up in a nutshell why you left—

R: Losing touch.

L: Right, you've said this before. You keep saying you feel celebrities need a rehab where they go to detox from fame. Because they're so out of touch they haven't learned the normal activities of life. Like never learning to parallel park.

R: Well, I'm not saying you never learn, I just think that when you're very famous, as I was, there are things you don't have to do that someone

11

else will do for you, and you will allow them to do them. And the sad thing is, you get to the point where you basically allow others to live your life for you. I mean, that's the bottom line. You're going out to entertain strangers while someone else is home raising your kids and it just feels like an absurd choice. Listen, I had six years of mainlining stardom and I left because I wanted to try something else. Being that famous becomes absurd, you're in high waves.

L: You don't realize how high the waves are until—

R: Until you try to make it back to shore. When you walk through a mall you hear people whispering your name. You're constantly hearing, "There's Rosie O'Donnell." What you have to do is shut out the noise, and in order to do that you have to start shutting out other things too and eventually it distracts you from your own spiritual journey.

L: So you want to do a book about why you left your show. Because, as you say, you feel you were mainlining stardom. You feel you almost, or actually did, get addicted. And over the past years, off the air, you've been, I guess, detoxing, and seeing what happens when you're not on screen anymore, when no one pays any attention to you anymore, when you have time to be with, and rediscover, your kids. Have you, in fact, detoxed?

R: Yes, I think I have. Now mind you, I have nannies . . . I have a wife, and two nannies. There are always at least three women raising four children in my house. It takes a village, I made a village of women to raise these four children. I have it easy—very easy; with fame comes wealth—help, access, and freedom. But I'm still the kid I was. Only everything's easier, cleaner, and better and I'm not looking at the world through the prism of a victim anymore.

Basically, I left my show in order to come back and feel the small moments as huge. You start to miss the small moments, the real parts of your life. You miss the kids' stitches and the soccer games and the first steps. Yes, I left in order to come back.

L: What are some of the skills you learned since you've left?

R: Parking the car. Just driving myself, I had had a driver for six years. My goal that first year off TV was to pick up my kids at school every day. In order to get a parking space, I showed up a half hour early every day. And that's how I met my friend Sharon. She too was early every day for pickup. She's very intense in a way that felt familiar. We bonded. She helped me with my reentry into the world. She saved me seats at the Christmas concert, reminded me which day I had to bring a snack. We went to the mall, to the sale days at A.C. Moore. Crafty Sharon, she helped me a lot. She helped me relearn some of the basic things in life.

L: Do you think you'll ever go back on air?

R: No. The gross excess of the whole thing, it became repulsive to me. My perspective got skewed. Now, mind you, there are times when it came in very handy.

But listen, fame is like a tattoo. It never goes away. Eddie Munster, Butch Patrick, now fifty-something—he was at a diner trying to get a cheeseburger and the waitress said, "Oh my God, are you Eddie Munster?" He can't get rid of that. It's a tattoo on him forever. I used to think the only way to get unfamous was to pull a Garbo and literally disappear and stop speaking to anyone publicly and go out in disguise. I used to think I'd never be unfamous in America because that show was too big for too long. Maybe no matter what I'd always be identifiable. Anyway, as for going back on air, that's not where I'm at right now.

L: So where are you at?

R: Home. I am home. Still doing foundation work. I'm opening a musical theater school in Manhattan. I'd like to get, like, ten rich feminists together. And each of us could give a million dollars. We could fund a feminist majority. It's such a patriarchy and we're so oppressed; we're raped as entertainment. On network TV. Terror—right here in the USA. Where are the women leaders? Shirley Chisholm—Gloria Steinem—Betty Friedan. It makes me sad. We seem to be going backward as a nation. So, I want to get the rich women in this country together, to start something by and for women and girls. It seems so simple to me, so obvious. So why doesn't it happen?

L: Good luck. I doubt you'll get very far.

R: Maybe not. But you asked. In these years, that's what I want to do, plus paint. And I've begun a blog, which is a whole new medium to explore.

L: You didn't answer my question: do you think you'll ever go back?

R: I honestly don't know. I do know I've been off air for four years now and I've changed a lot. That thing I said about fame being a tattoo. It's right but it also isn't right. Because the other day, you know, I was in Target, and this woman came up to me. She kept kind of circling around me, making me uncomfortable, and I thought, "She's going to ask me for my autograph." But she didn't ask. She just kept staring. Viv was with me, and I pulled her just a little closer to my side. And we were just about to leave the store.

"Hey," the woman said.

"What's up?" I said.

"Didn't you," she said. And then she paused. It seemed a long time before she spoke again. "Didn't you used to be someone?"

I smiled and said, "No. You have me mixed up with someone else."

She turned and walked away.

⌒

Blog 3/15/05

This is from a book I wrote but decided not to publish
Celebrity detox was/is the title

I am getting paid 2 million dollars for this book.
That's a lot of money.
Lauren Slater, the un known and un named one who is the
   brains behind my first book.
She turns a scrap of bread into a four course meal.
And without her there never would have been
"find me."

I called her up. I did.
Out of the blue—
Lauren Slater—
who wrote books that spoke directly to me—
a poet whose yellow is blinding beautiful

well this was my chance I thought—
the magazine—she will be the literary weight
she is how I want to write
I can learn from her
I dialed

she has never heard of me—
her kitchen is noisy and a mother is there—
but I knew from her books that her mother was not *a mother*
so who was this mother and why was she at the home of
    Lauren Slater—
a woman I had never met
yet was sure would never have her mother in the kitchen

Somehow it worked.
I trusted and she did—and push pull—
I was right—I get her—she gets me.
Her crazy is familiar and welcoming
with her I am not alone.

She has one currency
truth—the most important one.
She needs to bathe more
I need to lose some weight.

Anyway Lauren doesn't think I should tell you about
    the money—
cause you reading the book—do not now—nor will you ever
    be paid 2 million dollars for anything—

and it will come off sounding cocky or arrogant.
It is an unreal life I lead.

Eminem would rap it.
Cause he writes what he lives—
faults acknowledged—irony cherished.

I am rich.
Richer then I ever thought I could be.
it feels odd
It makes my life so much easier in every practical way—
but it doesn't change anything.

And I can hear it
"screw you bitch
I would gladly trade places
You think it is tough
And blah blah bah"

But folks—if I was you
and not me—I would want to know
From someone who has been there n back

you have it better—you do

It has been one year since my show ended—
I went to goosetown day school fair and ran the button booth—

and I was the field trip mother at the children's museum
with my 5 yr old—
and I know I have it as good as it gets.
So much help.
When I have had enough I go into my studio and paint.
I do
For hours sometimes

When my kids write their books
"MOREMAMA DEAREST"
There will be a whole section about my daily absences
from their life

I told kelli last week that the reason I became this
        successful—
I now think—
was cause I knew it was the only way I could parent.
With everything at my disposal—
I wanted ziplock bags—dixie riddle cups and lava lamps.
or I couldn't do it.
I am not that brave.

So I left my show.
I was offered 50 million to stay
unreal
everyone told me I was being an ass—
except kelli

And my life is better.
And my best friend is still Jackie and always will be.
I am happier then I have ever been. I am adjusting
I talk too loud in a group—
I cannot parallel park—
I try to control things I shouldn't—
I worry.

Celebrity is a drug
It is held up as the answer and never turns out to be.
ask joni—ask marshall

peace

CHAPTER 3

King Midas and Me

The day after the premiere, Barbara Walters called me up to see if I was serious. Would I consider being the fourth host on *The View*. "Yes," I said to her. "But I can only do a year because I don't know if I can handle it." What I meant by that: *I've built something solid here, something with Kel and my kids, something that has to do with daily life and the moments no one could ever put a price on, and I don't want to lose that.* What I meant: *I've spent the past four years in my own private cocoon, with my own ideas, blogging them and giving them away for free on the Internet. This has been my own private channel. For the first six months, before anyone knew I was doing it, it was especially glorious, because people would come and leave me comments. The dedicated ones found their way through the maze to get to the place where I had planted a tiny seed and it was starting to sprout for all the most fervent gardeners.*

So why would I want to lose these private places, these webs that were my own? I thought one year would be a way to strike a balance. I remember calling Elizabeth Birch, the CEO of my foundation, For All Kids, and telling her about Barbara's offer. And when I told her she said, "Ro, that's fantastic. That's absolutely the perfect stepping-stone back in. It's what you've been looking for and a one-year deal is perfect."

And I remember saying to her, "The show is over by noon. I could be in the car by twelve-thirty and be able to pick up my kids from school every afternoon."

"It's perfect," Elizabeth said again. "It's the perfect balance of family and work." And it seemed it would be. A mid-morning show, four days a week, someone else's signature on it. A show that didn't belong to me—it would give me a certain distance, and the freedom necessary to raise my family. I think this is close to every workingwoman's dream. It's the fantasy that somehow you'll land a gig that allows you to explore your talents without shortchanging your children, a job both big and small enough to allow you to exist in all your dimensions—domestic, corporate, maternal, artistic. In the beginning, for me, *The View*, or even the possibility of *The View*, was many things: a stepping-stone back onto air, a credible compromise between work and parenting, and maybe, above all, an experiment, the kind they used to do with alcoholics. Sober them up, wring the ether out of them, and then give them a small cup of scotch to sip. The question: could they sip or would they slug? *The View*—I thought I could sip.

⸱

Perfect. What's perfect? I have always chased perfection in everything I've done, and of course I've never achieved it. Perfect exists way out there, in infinity, and I've lived long enough to know that the stretching is what strengthens you. If perfect were a bird, it would die in domesticity. I was not searching for perfect—I didn't expect perfect—I was open for the adventure, to find out what I was made of—or not.

⸱

What I remembered: the studio lights, the audience, the seventy-year-old woman from Florida who waits in line in the middle of winter to see your show, and when she gets to meet you, takes your hand in hers, and her hand feels leathery, and also loving. Those women— strangers—so giving, so full of love; for me, it is hard to take in. I'd been cocooned away for four years and the thought of being *on air, in air,* it was appealing. But it also frightened me.

Myths

King Midas has riches, is propelled by greed and keeps craving more. A god of early Greece offers to grant him a wish, so Midas, who desires beyond desire, wishes that everything he touches turns to gold. He touches his child and is horrified to find she goes from girl to garnet, from a living child to a high-karat concept—his loss irredeemable, his grief living beyond language. I get the point.

~

Look at all the other artists, entertainers, who had had enough and then tried to take a second helping, only to have it all fall apart. I had so much, made so much, a nationally known figure of pop culture, and to hold out my hand and try to take more, it seemed innately dangerous, even rude. I was way out there where few surfers get to surf, and then I made it back to shore, put my board in storage. And now I was thinking of paddling back into that surf. What is the definition of crazy? This.

Supposedly there are some things you never forget, like riding a bike, or swimming. Some activities are so engraved in a person's gray paste that you can have a massive stroke and lose more or less every ounce of sentience, and become for all intents and purposes a breathing vegetable made nevertheless of meat, and need a wheelchair and a feeding tube, but if you're tossed in the old YMCA pool, you can still swim the butterfly, if you once could, way back when before your brain got busted. I'm not making this up; there are all sorts of stories about people losing all their faculties and abilities except for those they didn't: the deep abilities that could comprise what we'd call character. I know if I snapped a synapse I could still swim, but I didn't know that if I stepped off the stage I could remember how to go back on. Maybe I'd accept *The View*'s offer, and go back to TV, and find I couldn't do it anymore.

~

"No one in television gets a one-year contract," my agent said to me when I called her. "You can't do that, Rosie."

Agents really are in bed with the studios. They can't protect you fully because they have other clients who also need work on that same network. I told my agent once that I felt like the hooker, she the pimp.

Round and round we then went. I went round and round and Elizabeth went round and round with ABC. Understandably, television networks do not like to sign one-year contracts with people, because if the show works, they're left after twelve months holding the bag. This makes sense to me, but my intent was always my own. One year. It seemed to me to put parentheses, or parameters, around the gross excesses of celebrity-hood.

~

My own TV show started June 10, 1996. Around July the TV character Arthur came to open the new mall in our town. Parker, still in diapers, loved to watch Arthur, so I took him to the mall. Everyone there was looking at me and I remember thinking, "God, this is odd." A little bit of panic started. Arthur was late. People kept coming over to me as I stood there with my son, waiting for Arthur, and all the people were whispering and pointing and coming up. This sort of thing hadn't ever happened to me before, and the panic kept coming, so I left. I left with Parker, which was fine, because he wasn't yet two and had no idea Arthur was coming anyway. We went home and had mac and cheese and he went down for his nap. As soon as he was asleep I heard the gate ring. And when I went to look out the window I saw the top part of Arthur's head and his fuzzy seven-foot ears peering over my fence. "Hi! We heard that Rosie and her son tried to see Arthur at the mall but they had to leave so we came here!"

I was stunned. "Well," I said, "um, Parker is sleeping right now, but thank you anyway." It was awkward and I felt almost afraid, unsure. Something had shifted. No denying it.

People often ask me why I decided to leave my show. Well, Arthur rang my bell . . . that's what I wrote in my last book, the one I *didn't* publish, because I couldn't. Too early. Too true, and also not true enough. That book, which I also called "Celebrity Detox," was wrapped up with a red bow on its pretty packaging, when real life is scraps, held together by Mod Podge, messy at its edges. When I read through the pages now though, I see some things worth repeating:

Chapter One

People ask me why exactly I decided to leave my show, and I give them one reason: yellow.

Fame stole my yellow.

Yellow is the color you get when you're real and brutally honest. Joni Mitchell is my yellow. Bruce Springsteen. Cyndi Lauper. I have been soaking in them lately.

Yellow is with my kids—with Parker always—the boy who first handed me my own piece in human form—himself. The bundle of bright yellow warming my very core, formerly frozen and uninhabitable. Parker.

Fame stole my yellow, my time with my children, my true voice.

Broadway shows—they were the never-fail yellow station for me—"fill her up, high test," and in it would go as the orchestra tuned itself and the lights started to dim; yellow, glorious, life-altering soul fuel the life force yellow. Yes. Always on Broadway.

And then, in year three, I started to notice something was missing from my opening nights. The attention on me ruined it somehow. I started watching who was watching me, waiting for their response. I was no longer alone in the velvet seat—in the world of theater—I was being looked at. People watched me watch a show. It changed everything.

When I got too well known, then the joy of just watching people anonymously on a street corner was gone. The joy of finding the perfect cotton Gap pullover—size twenty-four months on the sale rack—no longer there. Playing with my son in the park while people stared—ruined. All of my yellow places started to fail me.

If you are good at stand-up, and I think I was—you make yellow. Chris Rock does. So does Ellen DeGeneres. They tell life's common experiences from their own truth point.

Truth. The truth. What is it and how much can you compromise it before it goes? I thought

I told the truth on my show. Year one and year two I did, at least to me. Enough truth to allow me the yellow. And it was there; the show was a hit. I spoke of my dream to see Tom Cruise and Barbra Streisand—I believed in their yellow; I saw it quite clearly. Here I was, an outcast, a fat Irish tough gal from New York, invited to the palace ball. And when that was real, the public responded. They got yellow from me, and I felt yellow giving it to them and it was all good. I was canonized the <u>Queen</u> of <u>Nice</u>. I was universally loved and praised and at first it felt good, but soon thereafter it began to change. You can develop a taste for worship.

It started to show then, on my face and body. I became bigger and sadder, starving for yellow, filling it with food, madder still at my expanding girth.

Since the yellow comes from living, the constant working makes creating that color impossible. What could I share with others when my truths were becoming more and more unreal? I fell in love—with a woman— yellow, a life-changing level of love, and then I forced myself to deny it. I reasoned with myself—I won't tell but I won't hide. And Kel came places with me and the press knew and

*it was printed but I never commented. I
thought that was okay, but it wasn't, and the
yellow we had together lost something by
never being let out.*

*So, why am I leaving my show? It took
my yellow. I wanted it back. Without it I can't
live. The gray kills me.*

I thought the greatest thing about leaving my show
would be growing closer to my kids, Parker, Chelsea,
and especially Blake, because he was just a toddler
when I left, and he didn't talk very well. He wasn't
acquiring language as fast as we would have liked, and
I knew it had to do in part with my absence in his life.
And I missed him, which was weird—it's weird that
you can miss someone you don't really know, but I
believe children can get almost immediately past the
place where there are barriers, and that a relationship
with a child is maybe the one, the only kind of sudden
click, or instant intimacy that's possible. After I had
finally freed up my life I took him to Chuck E Cheese's
and we played Skee-Ball. We went to the park; we went
skateboarding, and he started to find words: *water,
tree, see.*

Last year, before I started *The View*—before I was even asked to—Kel, me, and the kids went to the US Open. The stadium was named after Billie Jean King—feminist superhero, sister, friend—amazing. We sat in the stands with her. I was rather unfamous, so I was free, free to watch the ball, free to see my kids, free to talk to Billie Jean, whom I just love, truly.

Billie Jean is the real deal. It's like befriending your teacher in a way—no matter how familiar she becomes to me, I will always be slightly mystified that I am near her. And being near her, and thinking of her now, as I write this, I think (and thought) of all the women who went before me in the surf and inspired me to try.

Billie Jean King inspired me to try, for sure, walking onto the court with Bobby Riggs, a loudmouth old man tennis player who hated everything Billie Jean was. He called her names, taunted her, teased her; he challenged her to a game of tennis. There was no way, he claimed, she could beat him.

He was her Trump, Billie Jean's Trump, only Riggs had actual talent; Riggs could play tennis. He played. She played. Lights, cameras; everyone I knew was watching

31

that match. Out she walked with a baby pig, because that's what Riggs was, a male chauvinist pig.

And out she came, clutching that squealing baby pig. The crowd roared. The animal ran around the court. I remember this now. I remembered it then, there, sitting next to King. They started. And she had his ass all over the court. The woman beat the man. This was the beginning of everything for me, as a woman.

$\backsim$

Billie Jean King was mobbed that day at the US Open, with everyone asking for her autograph while I just sat there and watched. And it was a great day, a great thing, to be the observer, not the observed. I could almost feel my eyes, like lenses, open up and take in light, and color. I could tell you all the details, the fluorescent yellow of the balls smacking back and forth, the wind-whipped hair, Blake's new baseball hat, the plane overhead, its fuel scarring the sky in a line. I felt free and also tethered, finally, to the right place, to the right time; here. Now. These people mine.

Chelsea was less interested in the tournament than she was in the athletes. Blake and Parker were watching the tennis, and Chelsea, who was sitting next to me, got up and went on her own to the box suite, where there were all these amazing women gathered, tough-assed ladies in their seventies, sports enthusiasts, some golfers.

Chelsea apparently held court there for the entire time the match was going. She wound up sitting next to this beautiful blond woman who was showing her a book about female athletes. After a while I came over to see. "Who's this, and this?" Chelsea kept asking, and the woman was explaining who each featured athlete was. Amazing gymnasts, tennis players, and figure skaters. And they turned to a page in the book where there was a picture of a woman who had no legs—she was running with steel springs, her blond hair flowing behind her. The book explained that this woman was a champion. And Chelsea said, "What happened to her?"

And the woman said, "Well, that's me." Chelsea looked at the woman, and then back at the picture, and then back at the woman, her mouth partly open with surprise, concentration. And then the woman said, "I had my legs amputated when I was a child."

"Can I see?" Chelsea asked.

The woman said, "Yeah."

She pulled up her pant leg and showed my daughter where the prosthesis attached. They talked about why her legs were gone and how it felt.

It was a gift to watch this. It was a single moment, a moment so real you wish you had a camera to capture it, knowing somehow that if you did, you would taint it. I know the best moments can never be captured on film, even as I spend nearly half my life trying to do just that.

Maybe what it means to be an artist is knowing you are doomed to fail, that you can't capture your "it," because sometimes the feelings are so huge they go beyond your medium, and so you are left standing there, staring: your girl, one leg, two women . . . on and on the story goes, so much faster, and smarter, than you will ever be.

The woman, Aimee Mullins, ended up giving Chelsea the book and inviting her to a dinner of the Women's Sports Federation, where she serves as president. Chelsea was so excited. The tournament ended, the great day was over, and we went home and ate dinner at our local Mexican restaurant and then went to bed, but it was like the sun hadn't set yet and the good things kept coming—my life as a used-to-be, a washed-up woman, like the glass on the beach, beautiful glass, blue and green. Its edges softened from the sea.

And the sun didn't set on my day. It went on, in part because Chelsea could not stop talking about Aimee and all the women she had met at the US Open. All she wanted was to go to this dinner and be with these women. We went. They asked me to present an award. I said, "No, I'm going with my daughter. I'm going to sit down with my daughter and watch these women." And this is what I did. I watched and watched . . . for the whole four years I took off I exercised my eye, and tried to focus from angles I hadn't even known, or had forgotten existed, and the experience was a little like geometry when you suddenly see how shapes might come together, can come together, when the measurements are exact. I did a 180-degree U-turn and I wound up in a new place that was also, weirdly, a very familiar place where I was at once old and young, where I was who I used to be but also something new, and if I had to give this place a title, I would have to call it home.

ᕬ

I was with Kelli in Times Square when I saw the announcement go up: Rosie To Co-Host The View.

"Well, that's nice," I thought. "I'm glad I was the first to know." The one-year contract was still an issue, but it seemed we were going forward; it was clear we were. I saw the billboard in Times Square, and it was real. Inside, my thoughts: *"Prepare for reentry."*

ᕬ

I knew I had to hold on to the purity of my intent. I knew my intent was not to gain status, or money, or fame this second time around, but to be . . . groundbreaking.

Ruthie, my Kabbalah teacher, with whom I regularly meet, and who teaches me all things spiritual, told me my ego is my biggest fault and challenge.

Oy vey.

I wanted to go back because I knew it would be groundbreaking. One can break ground quietly; one can start a small crack or dent that does not mean much, except that it is an opening. When I started my show I was in the closet. There were no gay people on TV. Ellen wasn't out yet and there was no *Will and Grace*. Now here we were ten years later; I could do it all again—only be out. I would be able to talk about my family like the other hosts did. I thought, "Wow— this could be a big deal." I thought, when I saw the Times Square billboard, that this was what I was meant to do.

There are no mistakes.

Faith or fear.

Remember to breathe.

Maybe my job was to ride the wave, make it to shore, and rest. And then, once rested, surf out again, swim out again, only this time, without barriers or boundaries—without shame. Just be. Allow the light. Corny but true, that was my intent.

⌀

I have had tremendous luck in my career, amazing op-portunities to work with some of the best artists alive, and now another opportunity was coming my way. I have been fortunate. Almost all the directors I've ever worked with have been women, which is shocking to begin with, considering the law of averages. I got to be directed by Nora Ephron, Angelica Huston, and Penny Marshall. I have come to know and love Mia Farrow, Chita Rivera, Sharon Gless. Celebrity is odd—hard to make your way through. As I said, a few months ago Jane Fonda was at my house. Now I know people think celebs hang out with other celebs a lot—but I haven't found that to be true. Jane Fonda called me one day and said with sincerity, that she would like to know me better, be my friend. I invited her over and she came.

I'm the kid from Rhonda Lane, so how did I wind up here, or, rather, how did *she* wind up there, talking to me in my home? In the five hours Jane Fonda visited me, she was able to mine through all of my "movie-star mother" issues. And she walked down with me to my craft room and sat with me and watched twenty of the movies I had made, and looked at all of my art and asked me questions. Every fantasy I'd ever had about a mother being alive and wanting to know me came true, in that time with Jane Fonda in my craft room. And then we walked back up to the main house. Her son called and told her he had asked his fiancée to marry him the other night, and he wanted to tell her about it. I watched her eyes well up and I heard her ask about the ring, and, you know, I was thinking, "Wow." I had just watched her live a real moment in front of me and the fact that she is able to live and feel all of that is why she's a great actress, because most people can't take that in. That was a moment of near complete clarity for me, with her in my kitchen, and thinking of her sitting on a tank in Hanoi in 1972 and speaking of peace at a time when I knew that peace was the answer because children know; their souls are closer to God. She inspired me as a child and here she was in my living room continuing to inspire me.

~

This is what I was thinking in Times Square, when I saw the billboard, how lucky I had been, past opportunities, none of them lost, so why lose this one? Jane Fonda had been in my house and now Barbara Walters was asking me to be on her show, and it was startling to me, and the very fact of that—the startlement of it—made it clear to me to go forward. With the intent to challenge the image this country has of celebrities. The intent to work with very talented people. The intent to laugh and hear laughter, and not to get lost. One year only. I knew a person is only as good as her brakes, just like any other forward-moving machine.

~

In real life, which is not the same as a memoir exactly—in real life the billboard happened second, the Emmys first. But this is not how the telling has happened, not how the story seems it should go. Barbara was excited to speak of our future collaboration onstage at the Emmys, and I was excited to see her do so, to be on the stage with her when she made the announcement, because she is legendary, Barbara Walters. She is a weather girl who made one of the widest wakes in the history of the women's movement. She is, in this sense, a mother, or grandmother, to the many who have followed her footsteps. She has one daughter, Jackie, named after her sister, both of whom have been a source of private pain for Barbara. Throughout our entire relationship, I have always been acutely aware of both the public and the private facts: her struggles with her daughter and vice versa. She has told me I remind her of Jackie, whom she truly adores. Jackie has rejected the gold and glitter life: she lives in a small town in Maine, counseling troubled teens. Plain pain—in the end the only kind there is.

After Barbara asked me to co-host her show, I sometimes wondered about the daughter, and her hurt, and if she'd felt abandoned by a mother who was maybe so busy with the world that she didn't have time for her kid. I don't know. Women's choices. What I do know is that the knot between a mother and a daughter is always fraught, always frayed, you can depend on that. I sensed a raw place in Barbara right from the start; I could practically see it, the haze of her heart, glinting like an ornament, but not, real, beneath her silken blouses.

And so there we were on the stage at the daytime

Emmys, together. Because the news of our collaboration had already leaked, we did, instead, a bit of prepared banter. I said, "I just read on the Internet that you have something to ask me." The stage was hot, from the full force of the lighting, and below us I could feel the swell of the crowd. Barbara said, "Would you be on my show next year?" and I said, "It's either you or *Celebrity Fit Club*." This part we had planned, but then I swerved. I surprised Barbara, the same as many months later she would surprise me, and a rift would form between us, and within me a rift that would forever change the way I saw celebrities, myself included. But I had no way of knowing, that day, no way of anticipating all that was to follow: the abandonments, the dissembling, lies that lit the way toward truth, a new path for me, a total turn. *The View*. It changed my view forever.

But on that day, at that moment, we were just at the bare beginning. The conflict had not even started to simmer. I turned and I looked Barbara in the eye, like she'd looked me in the eye the night of my documentary, and said to her onstage, "Thank you for asking me, Barbara Walters." And Barbara Walters, she got choked up, and I think I saw the haze of her heart beneath her dress, and then she leaned forward, and put her forehead next to mine.

Blog 12/24/05

five and fierce
pins put in his busted elbow this morning
now—in bed next to me
his lips dry and cracked

a newborn waited
unaware
on the cot next to his
mother and grandma
crying beyond scared
too tiny—this baby
to go under and out
to have to fight so soon
for life—air
unfair

out of myself
gratitude
perspective
half-full

i cannot spell
i never could
commas and capitals
only in the way
on i go

unworthy
blogging
hmmm

who is the mother
we both say me
instantly
instinct

not of my body or blood
this brilliant boy
naming every animal
without a thought

the doctor comes in
i am not as famous now
but any fame helps
always
in emergency rooms

what did you do kiddo
he asks
broke my skeleton he answers
and my knees wobble
as my heart again grows

do i regret leaving
the razz ma tazz

queen of the world
they said
all of them strangers
my world
made up of 6 vital souls
that is the deal i made
my promise wish prayer

how selfless people think—say
no—i know—purely selfish
life perservers
each one
i took 4
knowing with them i could never drown

my boy will remember this day
his two mommies there
when terror shook all 49 pounds
soft songs sung

chances are i would have missed this
had i not jumped
i would have been at 30 thousand feet
hovering speeding across
to important and validating
saving strangers righting wrongs

lay down the cape

Rosie O'Donnell

two and 1/2 years now
i have been back here
at sea level
present panicked and plain
a mom
with watery eyes
nodding at the others
my sisters my friends

take care of your children
as i will mine

CHAPTER 4

Barbara's Show

In the right story, which is not the real story, my first day on *The View* is noteworthy, a grand return to daytime television. In fact, though, I don't recall much about it. What sticks in my mind are the precursors. I remember Bill Geddie, Barbara Walters's producer, coming to my apartment in New York City sometime during the summer before the season started. We have a little apartment and Bill is a very tall man, he's six foot five or something, a big guy, and a Republican. I'd hosted *The View* in the past, when I'd had my own show, so I knew what his politics were. I knew they were different from mine. Sometimes in the past I had even called him on them, in a sort of friendly way, like, "Why are we talking about lip liner when twenty-seven marines were killed in Iraq this week?" And he would say, "Because that's what we do on this show."

So, going in, I knew that we had very different politics, and this was a concern for me. I wanted to meet him first, to talk, and to make sure we could agree on how to make good television. After all, I'd never had a boss before, never in my life, in my career; certainly not in any traditional sense. There's real freedom in that but also real risk; you're on your own. No one owns you, and you don't own anyone. Those days are long gone, and while for the most part I'm grateful at how far I've come, how lucky I've been, I sometimes miss, or maybe just remember, the days way before I became who I am, the days when I had no worth, and yet, oddly, maybe more worth, because there's a purity to beginnings, to being unbossed, outside of any contract, your years your own.

I wondered what it would be like to be part of a team—that's what *The View* was, after all, a team—and as I wondered these things I recalled other things, the radical aloneness of being eighteen, in a time far before fame. I remember going up and down the East Coast, crisscrossing the country, making my way. Unbossed, radically free, and also alone, I did club after club. I got to know every airport. I'd land in a city and look for the guy with my name on a white sign. He'd drive me to the hotel, or the condo that the nightclub rented for the comics. Those condos, you can't forget them. They always smelled stale. They always had fridges with one leftover bottle of beer and a devilled egg with someone's mouth marks on it. Usually, the comic before, who'd been doing the city's circuit for a few weeks, hadn't paid the phone bill, and I'd lift the receiver to nothing.

The condos were lonely, and made more so by the smattering of personal stuff the prior occupants always left behind. I'd find the last actress' shirt in the closet, belted with sequins, or a used condom. Once I found a wadded up note, which, when I unfolded it said, "*Richard, go left out the drive and keep going straight till you fall from the cliff. Fuck you. Michelle.*" Michelle who?

But I wasn't depressed. I wouldn't say I loved it, but I had the sense of making it, doing it on my own, getting as much as $300 a week, which was more than I ever could have asked for. God, the gratefulness. Is it all gone now? I had two credit cards. I rented my own place in LA, for when I wasn't traveling. I opened a bank account in LA, with an ATM card to boot. In truth I knew nothing about banking. I just put in money. I never wrote down how much, where, when. I just deposited whatever I had and knew, since this was a bank, that everything would be taken care of. I trusted them, the bankers.

My method of money management was this: whenever I needed to write out some checks for monthly bills, I'd skateboard down to the Wells Fargo on Van Nuys Boulevard and pop in my ATM card. Balance? The machine always asked me. Yes, I'd punch in and it would respond with a figure: $782.92. Excellent. Thank you. I took the piece of paper back home and went to work. I went through my bills, in order of importance: rent, car payment, gas, electricity, Visa. All totaled $700. Lucky for me I had $82.92 to play with.

And with the stamped invoices in my chubby round hand, I skated down to the mailbox, dropped them in, and then quick cashed myself forty big ones. On the way home I would stop at the 7-11 for a six of beer and some pretzels.

A few days later, the bounced check notices would start arriving in the mail. Oh God, I'd think, not again. I made an appointment one afternoon with the bank manager. He wore a suit; I wanted to discuss with them the problem of their shoddy record keeping. I had facts and figures and a loose-leaf sheet with the balance receipt stapled to the top left-hand corner. This guy was toast.

I walked into the bank. There was a velvet rope with a tasseled edge. There were tellers behind panes of glass. The man I'd come to speak with was seated behind a big boat of a desk, and I could see his shiny shoes. He listened. I explained.

"Monthly, you know. It happens all the time. I get the balance, and that day write out checks, and you say I don't have it? Impossible. I have the receipt."

The man, listening to this, was stunned. He didn't move. He didn't laugh. He just stared at me. After a moment he asked how old I was. Twenty two, I told him, and I had two Visa cards and I was a professional stand-up comic; I had been on *Star Search*; in clubs; I was not someone who could have their bank messing up like this, month after month.

The man asked me to go over it again, my system, how I knew the mistake was not mine, the date on my balance receipt. I went slowly because he was having trouble understanding, which seriously concerned me, seeing as he was a bank employee. When I was done he lifted up my blank checkbook, with absolutely no notation of deposits or withdrawals, and flipped through it. The dry pages rustled. He took the loose-leaf paper with the ragged receipt stapled to it and walked into the belly of the bank.

"Heads are going to roll," I thought. "Someone is in deep trouble." After ten minutes, he came back out. "Okay Rosie," he said. "Listen, I'm giving you free unlimited checking, including a no bounce fee. You will no longer be charged anything concerning your checking account, as long as you agree to come to one training course on handling you account."

"Fair deal," I thought. I'd get to hold forth in the course about my superior banking methods, and in return, I'd get a no bounce fee.

So many people in my life have been nice to me. I see it clearly now.

The course was on a Sunday, at twelve noon. Everyone there was a Spanish speaker, except me. The teacher asked each of us how we recorded our transactions. Immediately I raised my hand and said, "I just go to the

ATM and see my balance, and then write checks for less than that amount."

The teacher started to laugh, really laugh, and then so did the students, who felt the funniness without understanding a word. I had cracked everyone up, and I wasn't even trying.

"That's a good one," the teacher said. "You should be a comedienne."

Well, I was becoming a comedienne, and the truth is, my act was getting better and better even if my banking skills were not. I could get an audience going. I was out there on my own. My own boss. I learned to write my own lines, and then I learned something else: not to write them, to just stand on a stage and let things float to me, sudden sayings, riffs and swerves, which is the best art and the best humor: unplanned.

❧

I didn't need to know a lot about Bill Geddie, or any boss really, to know that the whole point of management is planning. Bosses plan their company, their strategy, their time, their talk. At heart, I'm an improviser, not a planner. That's why I knew it would be a challenge to have any kind of boss, Bill Geddie or otherwise, but I knew I would try. I believed we both would. Despite the fact that he is a conservative and I am not, he also values human rights, so I knew there was some common core between us. At least I hoped so. Because this is what it's all about: a common core.

In the pre-show meetings that summer I felt the tensions of what was to come. These tensions are difficult to pinpoint in fact, but in my body they were not. Icy looks? Clenched fists? Tart tongues? No, not really, not then, certainly, when we were all trying our best to make it work. It was hot that summer, and I seemed to always sweat, because my body knew it needed to feel fear. I am a fat, loud, say-it-like-it-is-far-left-liberal while Barbara is a petite, poised, cautious, polite hostess. Why did we think the combination could work? Why did *I* think the combination could work? Simple. I wanted her to like me. Maybe even love me. Because no matter how famous I am, a part of me is always on the outside, too heavy, too hot, too damn much, at least for myself. Say it like it is, Ro. Okay. But God, it can be hard to hear.

I think I sensed what later became apparent, what later the media jumped all over: how upsetting I could be to Barbara, because I don't like scripts, or pretense. Much later on, weeks later, months later, I remember reading a newspaper report: "Walters was white" it said. The journalist wrote that the normally perceptive Rosie O'Donnell went on and on about money when, in fact, Walters does not like to discuss these things.

I sensed there were serious stylistic differences between me and the rest of *The View* right from the start.

They were as restrained and circumspect as I am garrulous and on edge. And then there's this. For six years I had my own show, ran things my own way, and these things reflected my beliefs at every level. My bottom line belief when it comes to almost anything is authenticity. If you are organic in your approach, you can be assured that good things will grow. On my show, I strove to say what was true for me regardless of its impact on advertisers or even the audience. When I said I loved Tickle Me Elmo, it was because I did, not because the company had some financial stock in that particular slice of airtime. It has always been of absolute importance to me to speak my mind, for better or for worse. Because I don't actually have a choice. It's my mind. It's not a car I can trade in for something slicker, or smoother, or sweeter. It's all I have to offer.

In the beginning, though, I had so much hope, so many ideas for the show. One thing I wanted right off the bat: the set changed. I wanted gifts for the audience. My belief is that the audience should feel welcomed, special; they are your guests. When you welcome them onto the set you are, in a very real sense, welcoming them into your living room, your home away from home, and they should be treated to creature comforts. The audience should never have to wait outside in the rain for a seat in the show. They should never feel thirsty; they should have a place to put their coats, rest their feet, sit softly. These things are important to me;

they reflect the real appreciation I feel for the people who take the time to hear me, crass, crap or cream, no matter. I like to give the audience gift bags, even, and we finally did that on *The View*; we finally started giving them big red bags inside of which were small simple things, but the message was big. *We care.*

I started out, in the preseason meetings and then on the show itself, with so many ideas and ideals and yet, no matter how much excitement I felt, it always sat side by side with my misgivings. I could not escape the sense, impossible to pinpoint but palpably real in the air, that while I was hugely welcomed as a co-host, I was also hugely threatening. I was too big, and that's true. I am. Then again, maybe I'm giving myself more credit than I deserve. Maybe I was more of an irritant than anything else. Or maybe my ideas were too cumbersome for them, and kept cluttering what had been, before my loud-mouth arrival, something simple and clear. I would suggest something and my ideas didn't seem to get the reception I'd hoped for, or maybe that was just my perception; no, it wasn't. Who has not had the classic dream of swimming against a current, or screaming only to see the sound shred to silence in huge winds, or this dream, my dream: trying to dial the phone, but not being able to move my fingers so there is, and cannot ever be, the satisfying click of connection. Often, at *The View*, or in the months before the show started, I felt like I was on a turnpike and each time I picked up some speed I'd get stopped at a toll booth, and inside there was a bored person holding out his hand in a latex glove. *Pay to proceed, please.* It was exhausting.

I wasn't used to this. My own show was syndicated, so I'd operated outside the demands of any particular network. The whole time I did my show I had only one person to talk to, Jim Paratore, the tall guy with the shiny shoes. I had this one go-to guy who knew me as I knew him, the communication clean. In addition, when I started my show I was not nearly as famous as I am today, so I was able to just have a cheeseburger with Jim and say, "Dude, this is how I do it, okay? I'm gonna try to give a hundred percent and we're both gonna make a lot of money and have a good show. And this is how I see it." Jim let me do everything, from the opening credits design, to how the set should look, to what color it should be; he let me do every single thing. I had total creative control.

When I remember the summer before the start of *The View* it seems the season was unusually hot. New York City is never a great place in July or August, but those preseason months seemed especially oppressive to me, the heat draped over the city, muffling the skyscrapers, melting the tar so it oozed and stank in the streets. In

Nyack, the roses bloomed for a brief period, flared pink and wine, and then the petals flaked off and scattered in the scorched grass. I smeared my kids with sunscreen as thick as mayonnaise but it never seemed thick enough, because the barrier filtering out the harmful rays had been so thinned from CO_2 that we were all essentially roasting on the racks—that's what it seemed to me. I was driven from Nyack into the city for these preseason meetings, and I always ran the brief distances between my front door and the cool air of the car, sprinted as though I were being chased by something fierce, and in fact I was.

One of the biggest conflicts, right from the start, had to do with the IFB, a device too tiny for the huge significance it held for us all. The IFB is essentially a gadget that you shove in your ear and that is connected, wirelessly, to the control room. They are used regularly on many television shows, from newsrooms to talk shows—day or night. I find this amazing, disturbing. The general point of an IFB on any television show is that, as you are talking to the audience, the people in the control room can also talk to you, send you suggestions and updates, feed you your lines:

MIRACLE HEALERS
A SPECIAL DATELINE INVESTIGATION
THE PREACHER HEALING THE ILL—
WILLING WANTING TO BELIEVE

INTO HIS EAR
CANCER—LEFT LEG—ARLENE
LOOK AT
RIGHT
THE TELEPROMPTERS SAYS
ARE YOU ARLENE
CANCER, IN THE LEG
SHHHH
THE RIGHT LEG
HOLD
COMMERCIAL BREAK
60 SECONDS
TIME IS RUNNING
RUNNING
RUNNING
SAY IT
ALL

"I'm not wearing an IFB," I said, almost right off the bat, because this was essential to me.

I CAN'T
I WON'T
I NEVER HAVE
I NEVER WILL
NOT ON LIVE DAYTIME TV
I AM NOT A NEWSCASTER

I AM NOT A PUPPET
NO

The IFB is not a bad instrument per se. It has an important place in broadcasting—IFBs were essential, I'm sure they were useful when the Twin Towers were falling and more information was pouring in by the minute. But in general, I don't believe it's a good idea to multitask talk. And as far as I'm concerned, I already have too much incoming. I have always been able to hear people conversing in the green room. I have always been able to hear extraneous chitchat around me; I have always been able to hear the buzz the camera makes when it runs, and all this sound—it is unbelievably tiring.

Barbara, I think, had a hard time with my IFB refusal. My guess is that to her, a former newscaster, not wearing an IFB is a very bad idea. "Nothing real can ever happen when you're wearing it," I explained. I don't think she bought it.

Feud Number 1: Kelly Ripa

Kelly Ripa had Clay Aiken on her show. Now, Clay Aiken, he's a young man, twenty-six maybe. He was a special ed teacher living with his mom before he became super famous. He's one of the biggest recording stars in the last twenty-five years, a real American idol. The world loved him. I watched as fame swept him into the pipeline—I was rooting for him. Gay rumors swirled around him—was he? Is he? The fact is, the public doesn't know what Clay Aiken thinks or feels or is because that's how Clay Aiken wants it to be. And that is as it should be.

So Clay Aiken went on Kelly Ripa's show.

What happened when he went on Kelly Ripa's show? It was clear to me that she didn't like him, for whatever reason. Some people do not click—they didn't. He had his Claymates in the crowd, holding up signs and screaming for him, and he tried too hard—and she was having none of it. So during some inane segment he interrupted and he put his hand over her mouth as a joke, as if to say, "Let me get a word in, kid, pass the ball, share."

And she said, "No, no, no." She spoke as though he were a child. And then she said, "I don't know where that hand has been."

And she took a condescending sip of water while making eyes at the audience.

"Low blow," I thought.

And Clay, he just crumpled up, like a little boy thinking he had done something wrong.

So I said, on air the next day, that Kelly's comment was homophobic, and she called in to the show, wanting to have it out with me on air. Which she did. They put her live on the phone. How dare I. I should know better. She has germaphobia. She likes gay people. I am irresponsible. Yes, well, okay. Got it!

But I am just saying that the whole incident looked to me like a gay person who had just had the gay card played on them.

That's how I saw it.

❧

The Kelly Ripa Feud was about many things for me: fairness, trust, respect. Would the Kelly/Clay incident have gone any differently if I was wearing an IFB? I say "no"—some say "yes."

Barbara I'm sure thought the Kelly Ripa Feud would have been avoided had I been wearing my IFB. I don't want to go through a long explanation of why that's not so. It suffices to say that Barbara just doesn't get it, my IFB hatred. She doesn't have to get it. She doesn't have to learn how to do improvisational comedy at seventy-eight or eighty-one or however old she is. She's a broadcaster, and when you're a broadcaster you use an IFB.

"What's it stand for?" someone asked me the other day. "IFB, what's that stand for?"

God, I don't know. I didn't know. I thought about it for a minute. And all I could come up with was this: *Inter Fucking fearing Bureaucratic bullshit.*

This is, of course, just in my opinion.

❧

"Like dogs sniffing each other." This is how my own producer, Janette Barber, describes the dynamics on the first day of the show. I can't say I experienced it that way, but I can say there was, perhaps, an element of cautiousness to the whole encounter. These women, after all, had been doing this show for what—nine years now—doing it their way, day in and day out, and then one day in walks the new kid on the block but she's not an ordinary new kid. She's the kid who comes to school in a Mercedes, the kid who is prince of some small island—you get it.

My intent was never to steal the show, my intent was to enhance it, but not all forms of help are experienced this way. These women had their own routines and ideas; I had mine. I've never done anything halfway. My own show won many Emmy Awards. I told Barbara *The View* would too. I am not sure she believed me. As for me, I don't have to have the prize but I absolutely must have the desire to win it—to set the standard and then maybe even go beyond. Without that desire, your limbs shrivel and your soul gets small.

A major conflict for me now, is how *not* to let my soul get small while doing mainstream television. Whether it's my own show, or whether it's a show I'm a guest on; whether it's here or there or everywhere, mainstream television has its limits, which is one reason why I sometimes think I should leave it, break out, and go fully into cyberspace, where there's a kind of radical freedom that frightens me as much as it appeals to me. On regular daytime TV, or nighttime too for that matter, the topics can lack heft. Girth. Weight. Who cares about Paris Hilton when what's happening in the world is happening? The fact is, the rift between television and the real world is often just so large that it's part of what drove me to quit in the first place. Here's my image, how I would paint it if I could: a pink and white room. Makeup artists swooping rouge on cheekbones powdered pale with talc. Topics that are at best irrelevant, at worst obfuscating the real situation we are in. My idea of television is that it reveals, not conceals.

My desire for fame was ignited in me when my mother got ill and died. I was ten years old then, and she died. She died first in our living room, lying on the couch in our house. She died later, and for good, in a hospital, alone, and she never ever came back home. Cancer. It grew in her body, cells swapping and dividing, but the details I have never learned; they were hidden from us. So much was hidden from us, for protection, for etiquette, the truth went up in coils of smoke from my nana's cigarette, surrounding her, and finally erasing her, my mother. This is one reason why, I think, I long for the truth, and more. I want to broadcast what's real, send it out in waves—silver sound waves lapping all over the globe.

How to pick a pet for your children. How to make chocolate mud fudge sticks using Swiss Miss.

Why Celebrity A hates Celebrity B. Why Celebrity B loves Celebrity A. What Celebrity C thinks of Celebrity A and B. Hot topics. Things that burn. Burns that scar the skin, peel away pink and underneath is new and too tender to touch. So much hurts here. Shhh. Don't say this. Shhh.

❧

I found this just the other day—a fragment from an interview I gave, to whom I can't recall, but they, the reporter I guess, must have sent me the transcript, and here it was, all of a sudden, in a file I can't recall filing. Sometimes you see your face in the mirror and it seems shocking to you. So too, your voice on tape or worse, pasted onto the page, where it freezes in its own hysteria, but there's some truth there, in the rambling:

I'm gonna start with 9/11.
Oh my God, 9/11 happens.
I was at the makeup chair
John McDaniel came in and he was crying
and he was telling me that
a plane had crashed into the Twin Towers,
AND STOP I HEAR STOP
and they know it's true
I can't believe him and I stand up.
Because if I stand up it'll change the reality

because I'm in control there, at 30 Rock
I'm the boss,
it's the Rosie O'Donnell show and I am, Rosie O'Donnell.
So nothing happens here that I don't know about.
Nothing!
Not a mystery guest,
SURPRISE BIRTHDAY CAKE
nothing
NOTHING happened on that show that I don't know about.
I was in control
I turned on the Today Show, Katie wasn't saying it
so that meant it didn't happen.
then I hear, "A tiny commuter plane has flown into the . . ."
"John it was JUST A tiny commuter plane"
then we see the second PLANE smash into that tower
live on television.
Live on television!
We watched an airplane full of families, people, human souls,
fly into a building, where hundreds of thousands of people,
innocent people, were just living their lives!
We saw it live!
On TV!
Well, that's when I knew,
"Check, please" I was done. I could not do it anymore.
I said "no"

I told them,
"I'm quitting! I am not going on,

I CANNOT go on television and do this show
when these kinds of things can happen in the world.
I CANNOT do it."
I didn't want to.
Because I wanted to be somewhere safe with my family.
I didn't want to be in the city away from them.
I didn't want that to happen again (crying).
I didn't want any more planes going into buildings,
I really don't but it happens every day,
every day, and there's darkness and I have to remember that.
There's darkness but there's light!
And the darkness is so powerful!
IT HAD ME IN ITS GRIP.
I went back on the air and I kept making my journals.
9/11 happened and I started gluing all the images from it onto
    canvas. my soul and my heart could believe it was true.
I was there.
I watched it happen.
But I still didn't believe it!
I didn't believe it was true.
So I kept gluing them and gluing them and gluing them.
Look!
I tried to trick my brain.
Look!
This is what happened!
YOU LIVED THRU THIS
(Phone rings)
There will always be darkness and

the trick is not to stay in the light
but ALLOW the light.
YOU ARE THE WINDOW
TRY TO ALLOW THE LIGHT TO SHINE THRU YOU
I KNOW THIS
IT IS MY GOAL
MANTRA
THE SECRET

Promise yourself there will be no more wars.
Promise yourself, start in your family.
It's impossible to fix.
That's not the way I wrote the script.
See the way I wrote the script is
this little girl goes through all this stuff
then she gets really famous
and she makes all the pain go away.
For her self and her siblings
she made it all better.
Well I got famous
and it didn't make it better!
And nobody wants to hear that.
Because it's a hundred dollars a ticket
and I don't fuckin' blame 'em.
I should shut the fuck up and deal with it myself.
9/11 happened so what relevance does all this star
    stuff have?
Zero.

OOOOOOOOOOOOOOOOO.
Print that on your page.
What's it look like?
Those are the mouths of people in planes,
screaming OOOOOOOOOOOOOOOOOOO
as they become bombs.
You can't change this channel.
there's no other show.
let's not pretend otherwise, okay?

(Back to music)

OOOOOOOOOOOOOOOOOOOOOOOOOOOOOOOOOOOOOOOO

For me, there is no pretending with a live audience.

I felt the energy of the audience that day. I felt very welcomed. I sat in the seat and everything went well. Janette tells me Barbara held my hand as we went onstage. That matters. It also matters that I felt my stage self come back. She had gone missing for four years; or, rather, I'd put her in storage, like you do the Christmas ornaments when the season's over, except the ornaments you know you can retrieve, while the second self—that's harder to find in the basement of the brain.

I was relieved to find her, relieved to lift her out and shake the dust from her clothes, relieved to see that if I turned the key in her back she could still sing and dance. I'm not saying she isn't real, this second self, this Rosie O; after all, Pinocchio was real. He didn't need Geppetto to make him so. He was real from the get-go, glowing green, the wood beautiful, burnished. My second self is dovetailed, routed by the best bits, every nail gold. I found her again, and it was as though she had never really left. People laughed. People clapped. Hello, America, I have always loved you.

Time is a strange thing. It's really not a thing. It's a concept. In childhood time moves slowly. My mother's illness seemed to take forever. In adolescence, time starts to pick up speed, like a lazy horse breaking into a trot, and by old age you're hanging off the mane as the stallion gallops toward the fluorescent finish line.

On air, time is altogether different from how one experiences it in any other parts of life. It moves faster than you can imagine, faster than you can feel. The first *View*, and every other *View* thereafter, was forty-one minutes on camera, but before you can say boo you are bowing out. I walked offstage. I had the feeling it had gone well.

Day two, the ratings came in and we were a hit. "Look at those numbers," I said to Kelli, I said to myself, I said the next day at work. I have no memory of anyone answering me; hello? Hello girls?! Look at those numbers.

I'm sure they looked. What I'm less sure of is how they felt.

Blog 9/5/2006

We went to a skateboard park
Finally

They have been asking for months

Saturday morning
Almost empty
Spray painted walls
Chain link fences
Ramps and lights
Thrilling

We paid for green bracelets
Padded up and headed out
Camera in hand
My deflector shield

One small boy
Maybe 7 zipped around
Curly hair glasses skinny adorable
Alone

His dad watched on the bench
Handsome boston college smart

We said hello and talked as parents do
Of r kids and their struggles

Which r ours
After
All

Half pipes r scary
U r sure u will fail

His boy
Showed mine how
Step down hard
Lean forward
Believe

Drop in
Dream and go
U can

Blog 9/10/06

week one down
nobody got hurt
the ratings r up
on we go

my torso is so long
i look like gigantor the spaceage robot
next to ms walters
they cut 3 inches off the chair
by day 2

parker finished 3rd
in a 10 mile race 2 day
i cried as he bolted thru the finish line
youngest runner they ever had
words fail me

tomorrow

5 years since
hard to imagine still
30 rock evacuated
we ran

souls shaken
as the city blew up
in front of disbelieving eyes

world sympathy poured in
the killing of innocent people
denounced by all
as evil

where r we America
the time is now
speak up

CHAPTER 5

$$$$$

The changes came right away. It was like flipping a switch. One minute I was a "didn't you used to be someone" someone and the next minute my face was spinning in cyberspace.

A few days after the first *View* aired, I turned on my computer and there was my face, on the front page of AOL, right next to a survey they were doing on whether or not something I'd said on air was ridiculous. There's a war going on, countless Iraqis are dead, and environmental scientists are predicting that the great polar ice caps are melting at a rate faster than they'd originally predicted. And what does this mean? This means, according to the experts I've been reading, that by the year 2100 flooding will be so severe many of our coastal cities will be washed away. And even before that, researchers predict, within the next decade we're going to see super hurricanes, like Katrina, fueled by greenhouse gases and pissed as hell, come barreling at us from out of the blue while walls of water suck human souls straight out of existence. And this is real. And this is true. And the Bush government—along with think tanks funded by fossil fuel companies—are launching campaigns to question what science has definitively proven: that we are alive at a unique historical period, and what we do from this point on will affect hundreds of thousands of years and the future generations consigned to life during those years—our children. Our children's children.

The government doesn't want us to know these facts. They want the pennies in their pockets now, and they're addicted to oil in a way that makes the sickest heroin junkie look healthy. What I feel in my bones is that the earth is at a true tipping point. I know people have been saying this since Homo sapiens became bipedal—*it's the end of the world; Christ is coming; it will rain birds and bats; a great gap will open up and the sinners will burn,* etc., etc. I know prophesies of catastrophe are as common and inevitable as drizzle in Seattle, but this is different. This is science. This is math. Dead Iraqis are a fact. Global warming is a fact. It is a fact that those of us alive in this slice of time stand at a fork in the global road, and many of us will live long enough to see the start of the devastation, if we haven't already. I have four children, and what mother could not but imagine their faces in the walls of water?

We have work to do. So when I see my face on the front page of a major news source and conduit of public information, next to a survey about some silly joke I told, I feel bad. Stop staring at me, okay? Why are you taking up so much space? And why are we talking about this when we should be talking about *this*?

So I could see, immediately, that my life was going to radically change. It was like flipping a switch and, boom, I woke up in Oz. But unlike Dorothy, I'd been there before, I've dreamed this before, and the lion, the scarecrow, the tin man, they're old friends of mine. Hello, fame. The chill, and the thrill, of déjà vu.

And that was the hardest part for me, plus how Kelli felt about it, even though she supported me at every turn. My children? Thank goodness they're not adolescents. What they know is that Mama is on TV; everyone knows Mama; wherever we go people want only to talk to Mama; we are not noticed, Mama is. They know she is a big mama. I worry that that, in turn, must make them feel so small. Which is fine when you are young, but it becomes less fine as you emerge into adulthood.

⟋

I know Elisabeth and Joy felt it too. Of course it was all over the papers: "Elisabeth and Rosie Fighting at *The View*," "Backstage Distress," etc. This was true, but only to a point, and that point ended far earlier than the media reported. But in the very beginning, yes, I felt as though Joy had her claws out; she was ready to pounce, and she did. Joy is older than I am, Streisand's age, and she didn't start as a comedian until she was forty, and she's funny as hell, I truly think that, so I have only admiration for her talent. But in the beginning she didn't know this.

Elisabeth, antiabortion, pro Bush, pro war, believes in everything I don't, and I believe in everything she doesn't. She's as slender as I am fat, as restrained as I am vociferous, as polite as I am frank. She's the Emily Dickinson poem incarnate, "Tell all the Truth but tell it slant/Success in Circuit lies," while I'm the Dylan Thomas poem incarnate: "Do not go gentle into that good night . . . Rage, rage against the dying of the light." Elisabeth. I can tell you this. Right from the start I could see in this slip of a girl so different from me, I could see something fierce, a fist in the frill, and I liked that. But we had no language in common.

If we had a language in common, perhaps we would have found our way to a connection sooner than we did, but I doubt that. Because, personality differences aside, there was always the fame problem to contend with. There was always the sense that by introducing me into *The View*'s configuration, you were shifting the pyramid's building blocks, giving it a point it hadn't had before. Fame is the ultimate expression of hierarchy.

And hierarchy is the ultimate structure on which anger, jealousy, and humiliation hang. How, therefore, could this have been easy? I know what it feels like to feel less than. No matter how great, how rich, how brilliant, how fat, there will always be someone else with more. This, perhaps, is the hurt we humans have never learned how to hold.

The Dream

I might have been eight or nine, at that age when your dreams are so vivid you sometimes fear falling asleep. The age of night-lights and worlds beneath the bed. And one night I went to bed and I had a dream that has stayed with me forever, a dream so palatable I could practically taste it on my tongue when I woke up.

My mother was sick and I knew it. While my father hadn't ever actually told us the nature of the illness, I knew she was dying. It was then when fame came to me as not a possibility but a necessity. With fame came money and with money came cure.

My dream was more like a picture than a dream, because the images are so still, so defined, so Crayola bright. I saw a swing set, entirely unoccupied, each swing moving with the wind, suggesting sadness, and spirits. I saw the sky, enamel blue and perfect. I saw the grass, every blade just barely curved, and the grass too was moving. I was there, kneeling by the sandbox, scratching in the sand with my fingers, feeling before seeing the coolness of coins buried there, sweeping the grains away to find handfuls of silver and copper coins— money! A lot of money! The distinct feeling of much- ness, because this wasn't just one or two pennies, this wasn't a stray nickel or dime, this was a gaggle, a flock, a brood, a litter of little coins that were now mine. I felt indescribably *lucky*. I felt the way you would feel if you were a miner trapped underground for hours or days, and suddenly you see the first crack of light when the stones are moved to show the sky, a helping hand. I felt *reprieve*. It was not greed. I felt relief, which is the best, most powerful, most intoxicating emotion there is—not joy, but the long longed-for absence of pain or fear.

That dream has stayed with me and is emblematic in my life, the hook on which I hang the explanation for many of my pursuits. Part of me has always wanted to make art, but then also part of me has longed simply, and primitively, for money, because it equaled from a young age the possibility of life over death. And you don't have to have a mother dying from cancer to make this equation. You don't have to have anything except citizenship in the United States of America to learn the lesson that money does not grow on trees; in our coun- try *money is the tree itself*. If you have money, you have life, you have air, you have leaves and shelter and wood and the possibility of being a planet, a star in the sky.

A significant percent of lottery winners are broke within four years. Something like 75 percent of them develop an addiction or a mood disorder, like depression, that they never had before they won their loot. I'm not here to say money is the root of all evil; it has allowed me to live a kind of life that is so incomparably easier than it would have been had I, say, been a schoolteacher, and for that I'm very grateful. I see all it's done for me. When I know that if any family member or friend is sick I will be able to get them the care they need. When I know I will never have to worry about retirement, or whether my kids can go to college. When I know I don't have to worry about paying my bills or getting that loan. When I know that if I get the flu at the same time as my kids, I won't have to do what almost every mother in America has probably had to do at one point in her life, puke in one bowl while she holds her kid's head as he pukes in another. Sometimes I can't imagine how people do it, real life, and I believe perhaps it's good that I have the money, because maybe God knew I didn't have the mettle to make it through without.

That said, I also know money is not the tree of life. It doesn't take away from the bottom line. There are too many things in the world that are just immutable to money. You can throw all the money you have at these things and they don't flinch. Money doesn't touch depression. It doesn't alter shame. It doesn't trump death. There's a researcher who did a study on how money affects people's happiness. He spent years studying this subject. What he found is that up to a certain point, money influences quality of life. Rank poverty lends itself to problems in health and education. But on the other end of the spectrum, he found that very wealthy people have actually *more* mental illness than people who are middle or working class. My question: why? Does the money make them mad, or are they so mad to begin with that they operate under the misguided notion that money can solve the problem of their own mortality. In my case, the answer is both.

⟡

My face was on AOL, next to a survey, while the world was warming and the war was going on. Kelli got her hair cut, and I saw her eyes in a new way. I went from being a slacker artist who spent all day painting in shades of yellow, to a prodigal celebrity who had to be up at six and out the door by seven. In the flick of a switch, yes. People began calling, writing. Some I knew. Some I didn't. Some were in trouble; some I had already helped in the past, and those it seemed to me I'd already saved; in my mind I'd done enough and what happens is people still want more; it can feel boundary-less, and you say to yourself, "Wait. Wait a minute." But I don't feel angry in the face of people's needs, or even demands. It just confirms for me that everyone has the same misguided fantasy that out there there is some person, or green bill, that's going to change everything and set it all straight.

But to be that person, to be seen as any sort of savior, that can take its toll. I went to the US Open with Kelli and the kids before *The View*. I did my own hair and we had a great day. For almost two hours Chelsea talked to the woman who had had her legs amputated and looked through the book of women athletes and totally loved the whole experience. We ate pretzels and had hot dogs; I had Blake on my lap and Parker next to me. And Kelli was sitting behind us with Billie Jean King and the whole family had a great time. Then we went back to the finals two weeks later and my show had been on for four or five days, and it was horrible. I was now one of the observed. They put me on the monitor with Jim Carrey who was there with Jenny McCarthy and all the other celebrities that you could watch; everyone looked to watch where the celebrities were, and I realized I had become one of the people that got looked at, and when that happens, you cannot observe accurately because you are the observed. And it's a trap.

Noise. And you know, I was sitting up there and worrying what clothes I was wearing and if I looked okay and watching people look at me and nod and then ask for my picture and the autograph. And the ones with frowns on their faces that I knew didn't like who they thought I represented or who they thought I was—to them I was the enemy. Terrorist even. Traitor. And then other women, came right over, saying, "Hey, how's it going, Ro?" as if I had gone to their high school, and I responded in kind because that's who I am.

After the matches we went to dinner at an Italian restaurant in Queens. A woman followed me into the bathroom. She could see my feet in the stall and I could see hers as she stood by the sink. "Rosie!" she said. "My name is Phyllis, I'm gonna wait! Take your time, honey! But I'm out here waiting! When you're done, I'm gonna give you such a hug! I'm gonna give you a squeeze!"

And what I was thinking was how was I going to poop in this situation. My whole life was ruined because there was not a private bathroom in my dressing room at *The View*, so now I could not go poop until I got home. I am not a public pooper. I never have been, I never will be. So my entire digestive system was now in a tizzy because I had nowhere to poop at work. I just don't understand; it's like they think we're camping.

Finally, I came out of the stall and saw her. Her hair was gray, and it was eight inches above her head and she had it in a clip, and her eyes were a little off. "How are you?" she said. She had no idea she was a poop preventer. "I'm Phyllis," she said. "Look at you! Back on the show! Looking great!"

We hugged, Phyllis and I. I indulged her. I took it all in, steadied myself on the surfboard, hoping all the while that I might make it through this new rise—fame.

CHAPTER 6

Letter to My Brother

Eddie:

There is no way I can stay on this show. It is everything I am not. It's called *The View*, but that's a misnomer; it's really a view, one view, ABC's view, and I'm not a parrot or a puppet.

When I had my own show I expected 100 percent from myself. And I expected 100 percent from my staff too. But *The View* show has already been set up in a way where the staff is not inspired or rewarded.

It's a difficult situation, because I got hired to do a job, I came, I did the job, I delivered, but I'm still not accepted here. I'm never going to be accepted here. It's not my show; it's nine years of someone else's show; it's a culture I don't understand and it's one I don't agree with either. I can't grow here. I

83

have to grow. What other choice does one have? You either grow or you die.

The director. He's able to make music look really good. Sometimes he's spectacular, to a level that awes me when I watch it. And yet, he's inconsistent. Everyone is; I know I am, for sure. How is it, I wonder, that a man who is able to do such spectacular work sometimes gets such murky shots? I've counted his cameras. I've watched him closely. He is tense, tightly wound. Art has to come from someplace quiet. Even when it's raging, when it's rageful, it comes from some still place inside you, someplace hard to get to, harder still to stay. I wish he could find that quiet place.

Listen, Eddie. It's hard. And that's why it's no one's fault. They've been making doughnuts at this factory for nine years. And people have been buying the doughnuts and everybody was happy with the doughnuts. So I'm not one to say, "You can't make doughnuts that way." But it's not the kind of doughnut I make, and it's not the way I make them. I'm gonna tell Barbara after Christmas break that I'm not going to sign on next year because I can't. But I've had a great time, and thank you, but let's not turn this into a negative because it isn't.

In the middle of the show yesterday, the lights went on, like it's last call at a bar. Every light in the studio went on, bright. I said, "Whoa!" For about ten seconds the lights were on. Afterwards I wanted to say, "What was that?" But I wasn't sure anyone would answer, or, if they did, tell me the truth. Oh, a glitch in the computer. A DC power surge. Could be this. Could be that. Thing is, Eddie, it seems to me that no one really cares.

I wonder why I care especially because it's not my show, which is maybe the point, and problem.

I just want it to be what it can be. I want the fucking IFBs out of everyone's ears, everywhere, not only here, but on every network; make TV live, truly live. All of us doing talk shows, acting, delivering the news: whatever the medium, it's important to make TV what it can really be. And to do so requires those who sit on my side of the screen to hear, to listen, to stay present.

And Barbara. At some point, a person gets tired. It's inevitable, the aging process, I can feel it in myself. My eyes aren't what they once were. Barbara Walters is almost twice my age and she's been doing this for nearly half a century; at some point it becomes necessary to step back. I hope when the time comes for me to do this, I will be graceful and go. Everyone has to go. Going is part of the gig.

And I'm sure it doesn't come easy for Barbara either. Who am I to say? I can only say what I see, feel what I feel. I feel, sometimes, her tiredness. I would like to tell Bill Geddie about her tiredness. I would like him to feel her fatigue, be in her bones; I'll bet it hurts there. I'll bet behind the glam and glitter it hurts to be Barbara, sometimes, because, while you can hide aging, you can't erase it; it leaves its grainy footprints, its smears. I want to tell Bill Geddie this. I want to remind him that he has worked with her for twenty-five years. His whole entire career is with and for and by her. And does he think with her legacy that it is still in her best interest to do live television? Does he even consider this, or is the profit too pretty? Maybe it's time for her to take a break. To go off the air, find the ground, sit down. Rest. She deserves that; if anyone does, she does.

The point is, Eddie, it's hard to be here, to watch this happening.

And I would be less than honest if I were to say that there is no trouble between Barbara and me. I mean, our differences are obvious.

During the commercial, people scream, "I love you, Rosie," and Barbara tells them in a schoolteacher tone, "It is impolite to say I love you to one person when there are four of us up here." Then a stony silence sets in. There are many rules I don't understand.

Once I was visiting Georgette Mosbacher and some fund-raiser guy, also visiting, told me about a new hospital for vets, for amputees from the Iraq war, and how these soldiers were not getting good medical care. And the fund-raiser told me his agency had already raised $5 million for these men, this hospital. "Did any celebrities give?" I asked him. "Yes," he said. "Cher gave three hundred thousand."

"I will match Cher's gift," I said to him.

Barbara found out about this. I could sense she thought I was crazy or just plain overboard. I must seem all excess to her, even in giving.

Here's the thing. I believe that people of substantial wealth, wealth of the sort that it appears to me Barbara has, and that I have, are called upon to give substantially. It makes no sense not to. If people as wealthy as celebrities such as Barbara and myself gave away half of our net worth, we would still have plenty left over, and we could actually save millions upon millions of lives. To not do so seems wrong, if not downright sinful.

I'd be a liar if I said I do not stand in judgment of those who disagree. I do. It is small minded. Greedy.

I need to try harder.

What I've learned: rich is not as much a fact as a feeling. Because no matter how much money you have, the thought of parting with half of it can seem devastating, when in actual practice it would change your life, your access to resources, not one bit. I try to remember this, and stretch each year just a little farther. If I want to give ten thousand, I ask, "But why not ten hundred thousand?" And indeed, why not? What will change in my life if I do this? Nothing. What will change in the recipient's life? Everything. Looked at from this point of view, withholding seems cruel.

Barbara I doubt would agree. So, no surprise, we see things very differently, Barbara and I. But the biggest differences aren't money or clothes or what have you. Bottom line, she's just not an entertainer. And she shouldn't have to be. I don't want to push Barbara to be something she's not. It's her show. This is her parade. I'm going at a different tempo. The ratings are up, which pleases her. But from a personal perspective, I think I've been very hard for her to handle.

My relationship with Barbara sometimes makes me wonder what it would be like with Mommy now—if we would get along, if we could find our way to friendship, to a mutual respect.

It's all about sharing, Ed.

Call me later,

Ro

CHAPTER 7

Who's Real?

Who's real? In celebrity land it can be hard to tell. Of course, this makes sense, because celebrity is in essence a mirage. It's the pool of blue water you see as a dot in the desert from a great distance, a dot that gets larger and larger as you get closer and closer, looking ever more luscious, until you cross a line you didn't even know was there and, poof, Houdini waves his famous wand, the crowds cheer and jeer, and—the water's gone. And what is it you then hold in your hands? Sand, of course. It's sand.

How would I know this if I am the celebrity and not the celebrity watcher? This is a good question. How can the mirage reflect on its own reflection? From my earliest memories I was practicing for fame, dusting my icons daily. There was Lucille Ball, Bette Midler, Johnny Carson, and of course Barbra Streisand.

I wonder if it is possible to love an icon. And I also wonder what the difference is between love and adoration. The celebrity I most, hands down, adore, respect, admire is Barbra Streisand. In fact, one reason I took the job on *The View* was because I knew she was going to go on tour, and I figured if I were back in the boxing ring, so to speak, I'd get great tickets to her concerts. I first had Streisand on my show in 1997. She wrote me a note a few days before she was to appear. "Are you sure you're ready for this?" the note said. "Is it all going to change?"

"Yes," I wrote back.

Streisand came on, the cameras were filming me meeting my dream in flesh, my fantasy in life, which is also, without doubt, death. And Streisand wanted to protect me from that, from my own disappointment and from its being aired to millions across the country. Only here's the thing. I wasn't disappointed; she retained her glory up close. She came close to perfection, and in the coming years would come closer still. I found her to be everything I had dreamed—and more.

I have read that children who lose a parent early never go through the inevitable process of parental disillusionment that is so essential to growing up. When you are very young, your parents are the tallest trees; you look way, way up, and thirty thousand feet above you, so it seems, are their round faces floating amid blobs of light and shadow. Maturity perhaps can be best defined by the diminishment of distance between you and them, until you eventually realize that they are just life-size people, flawed and fragile, and yet you love them still.

I know about this journey, but have I ever taken it? My mother died before I could take the trip to the tree-tops, to the moon, and back. I remember Neil Armstrong's trip to the moon, and how he saw, along with the rest of the nation, that whatever was up there in the night sky was not a piece of cheese, or a man in an orb, or a pearl on a background of black velvet. He saw what was up there as it was—a stark and severe beauty. My mother died. Sometimes, I wonder if she took with her my chance for transformation. Because I still see certain people as a child does. This is a great gift. A profound problem. A religion.

Our country is more religious now than I have ever known it to be. The other day I read in the *New York Times* about the controversy over a recent children's book that mentions on its first page the word *scrotum*. Certain people, among them librarians, are claiming that for this reason the book should be banned, because children must not read such words as *scrotum*. A body part. No different from *arm* or *eyebrow*. We can lasciviously pour billions of gallons of CO_2 smut into the real air, thereby ensuring that our children grow up on a wasted planet, but we are too prudish to allow them exposure to a normal human body part. Methinks the gentleman doth protest too much. About the wrong things.

Here's an example. Jim McGreevey. Remember him? He was the governor who was disgraced because he had an affair with a guy he put on his payroll as the head of homeland security for New Jersey. At the time he came on *The View* there was a lot of controversy in the gay community as to whether or not this man "helped" or "hurt" us because he used gayness as a smoke screen to deflect attention from his very unorthodox and possibly corrupt administration. Many were offended by McGreevey, offended by the fact that he had had sex with a guy and therefore likely endangered his wife and, to make matters worse, brought this man to the house while his wife was having a C-section: slimy stuff, no question. McGreevey's explanation: that being a closeted gay makes you act weird, that the weight of the repression drove him mad sort of thing. He used the cultural prejudice against gayness as an excuse for his poor judgment.

I had read his book before he came on, and it seemed to me like he was the typical nerdy gay Irish Catholic kid. I know fifteen of them from my neighborhood. They couldn't come out, and now they've come out, and I've seen the story; I get it.

He came on *The View*. He was well dressed, groomed, buttoned up. His shoes were shiny. I thought to myself "What are the chances this guy will give me the truth?"

On air, I sat back. Some were hoping they'd put McGreevey on live national TV and I'd call him a slimebag and chastise him for getting away with it all by using the gay freak flag as a defense, but here's what was in my mind: a lot of guys do just what he did to their wives with another woman, and no one cares. So why, when it's with a man, does it become a crime? That's what I was thinking. I didn't say it though. I kept that quiet.

I let Elisabeth ask the questions. She had many. They got into a predictable brawl, which was probably what everyone really wanted, because some tend to think brawls make for good TV. I disagree. At one point during the "debate" I interjected and tried to explain to Elisabeth the point McGreevey was fumbling for and he said, "Wow, you said that well. I wish I could do that."

I turned to him and said, on live TV, "You can't because you speak like a politician, not like a human being."

That's my whole point. *Like a human being.*

The rest of the show I don't really remember. The phrase "like a human being" kept repeating itself, as does the ticker tape at CNN. *Like a human being human being human being human being.* Weird words. A human. Being. Being what? That's what I'd like to know. Being who?

⟳

When Streisand sings, I feel myself begin to be. Her voice, so resonant you don't realize until you hear it that you have forgotten you are in existence. While it may seem strange, the idea one can forget one is alive is true for me, and I believe for others as well. There is so much sheer *stuff* to get through, so many interviews, appointments, tasks, books, talks, projects, meals, meetings, so many roles to play—mother, wife, friend, activist, philanthropist, comedienne—that one becomes a what, not a who. I become *what* I am doing, and that *what* flips as fast as the pages in a book, shape shifting, slippery. I have a friend who told me she gets so busy she forgets to breathe. As for myself, I can go hours, days, weeks, months, without any sense of my is-ness, instead becoming a series of tasks checked off. Next! Next! Next! This is a shame. It may even be a sin.

When Streisand sings it's a physical feeling for me, a welling up of things that are gorgeous and yellow. I listen and think of my mother listening. She is lying on the couch in our living room, creaming Nair on her legs, skinny with sickness, Streisand seeping through the pores in the radio on the shelf. She is standing by the window in our kitchen; it is May, and early, the day wet and blue, Streisand singing a sadness she has no way of speaking. Streisand's voice filled the house on Rhonda Lane, and it filled me as well, and became a substance that was soothing, a sound I could return to when the going got bad, when my mother died. I listened closely, the same way a burgeoning scientist studies his first glass slides beneath the mail-order microscope he got for

Christmas. I listened at my desk, in bed, at the breakfast table. Hers is a voice that you can break down into pulse and wave. Hers is a voice that proves sound has segments—flecks of color, scents of tang and soil, blood and mineral, memory and sadness, hands-holding. The voice stirs your soul and demands you to sing along. I find it odd and obvious that incurable stuttering can be cured through singing. The brain switches over. It is impossible to lie when singing. It is impossible to be anything but a *human . . . being.*

Ninety-nine percent of celebrity worship is built on illusion. Ninety-nine percent of celebrity culture is false. Streisand's genius is that she demands you to exist in real relationship to her voice. Streisand is not about distraction from the self. She is about a return *to* that self. When you hear her sing, you are brought backward into memories and forward into all you might be able to be if you could just catch the courage. *Courage.* A word I like. It comes from the French word *coeur.* "Heart." Streisand has a heart. My heart, a nation's heart. I wanted to film the heart's collective beat and give it back to her as proof of what she has to offer. I began to make arrangements with my producer Jen Le Beau to gather the equipment. We wrote to Streisand's people and asked for permission to film her fans outside the concert halls, to interview them and get on tape what it was they felt for this singer, actress, and activist. I envisioned the movie I would make, the gift I would give her.

I thought about proposing to *The View* the idea—stalking Streisand segments. Unlike McGreevey, this was the sort of stuff that would have really had meaning for me.

〜

I wanted to ask about a stalking Streisand segment, but on the other hand, I was feeling a "what's the point" exhaustion. I could hear them saying no; it was out of bounds for them. And it was just around this time, the time of wanting to suggest a Streisand segment and feeling so pessimistic about their response—well, just at this time I felt things start to shift a little in myself. One of my concerns was losing balance, caving in to the crowd, becoming an emblem or an icon to even myself. Starting to see myself as I was seen, which is larger than life, and therefore dead; celebrity culture can kill you. I would learn this later all over again, and in the worst way, when Anna Nicole Smith died. In some awful way, her death was not a surprise. It was a confirmation of things I already knew.

But I'm ahead of myself here. Anna Nicole Smith was still very much alive. And the pace of my life started to pick up dramatically. As I slipped back into celebrity land, the tasks multiplied a thousandfold, and the letters addressed to me but having nothing to do with the real me—the mother me, the married me, the friend me—the letters addressed to the celebrity me began to pour in again, asking for money, for help, for salvation. I had gone for four years living alone, and now my mailbox was overflowing and people were telling me I was fantastic, the funniest, the happiest, the brightest, the est-est of the ests; people were talking about my comeback as though I were not a person but a sport, and when enough people speak of you, and see you, in a certain way, you can become that which they think, or speak, or see. How to best explain this? It is a shift that happens in the head, and that very few celebrities will ever really speak about—the inflation of self, the pride. One begins to believe in the specialness, and a dangerous sense of entitlement takes over. It feels shameful to speak of, and I do not do it easily. The drunkenness is not from alcohol or morphine; it's from the steady stream of praise pouring in.

How did it manifest? In just the subtlest ways, like the inability, or unwillingness, to wait in line. The need to get my groceries, my tickets, my gasoline, my art supplies, immediately. Let me put it this way. Life is full of red lights and stop signs. When celebrity addiction starts, you become impatient with, even angry at those necessary obstacles. You think you could run a red light, or two. And then you do.

And there were other signs as well. I took *The View* job in part so I could have balance in my life, not be swallowed up by the demands of a career. Because the show was over by noon, I figured I would be able to pick my children up from school. During my years off screen, I picked my kids up all the time. I stood at the curb with all the other mothers, and made friends. At first, everyone was shy, but as time ticked on, and the years passed by, the other mothers began to forget I was Rosie O'Donnell and they came to think of me as Ro, another woman picking up her children at the end of the day. I loved those moments with the other mothers, worrying about grades, or who was misbehaving, or what the third grade teacher did. Sharon became a good friend. We worked out together. We discussed this and that. We waited in the dampness and the drizzle. We waited in the slush and the snow. We watched each other greet our hearts at 3:00 p.m. every afternoon, swooping the child up, each reunion as rich as the first one, this ritual important. I didn't want to lose it.

But as September slipped by, and as autumn tilted toward a creeping coldness, I began to miss the pickups, because I got too busy. There were meetings in the city, there were fund-raising events or phone calls or crises or I was just too damned exhausted to get the car going, to weather the weather outside. First I missed one afternoon pickup; then by early October I missed two or three a week. I craved time alone, time where words were not necessary. I spent whatever slivers of free time I had in my craft room, which overlooks the Tappan Zee Bridge, jeweled with lights that come on ever earlier as the darkness settles like a dust cloth over the town of Nyack. High up the hill, I could hear the car leaving, and I could hear it coming back, the sound of my kids as they tumbled from its heated interior and raced toward the main house. *Go up there and greet them, Ro.* Sometimes I did. Other times, though, I did not.

◦

The time for filming the first Streisand concert was coming closer. And I knew I was going to make this movie regardless of *The View*'s interest in its creation as a possible segment. "What would we get out of it," I could just hear them ask, because they might not know the obvious. Ratings, guys, ratings. But they didn't understand much about how to get ratings. In all likelihood, they'd decide the story had no place on their show, but that didn't mean the documentary itself needed to die.

Kelli, however, didn't want me to do the Streisand documentary. She thought it was a bad idea. I was already booked to the gills, and now I was planning on jetting from city to city, red-eyeing it back to Manhattan in time for live *View*s every day at 11:00 a.m.? Barbara Walters from the start saw my love of Streisand as more of a silly obsession than anything else. Other people simply thought that logistically I couldn't film every concert while maintaining my career commitments. I knew what I needed to do though. I knew filming Streisand was not a further departure from myself; it was, instead, a possible route of return. Therefore, it seemed obvious to me. I had to do this, as a mother, as an artist, as a person.

Jen Le Beau and I gathered our gear. We talked. We planned. "A love letter," I said to Jen. "Streisand needs to know the impact she has had on this nation." The more we talked, the clearer our goals became to us. A love letter, yes, but then more. By documenting Streisand's fans, by capturing their words on camera, their faces on film, we thought we could weave together a portrait of this country in its highest hopes and deepest dedications.

~

As I said, time in celebrity land blurs and blends. Days flip past like cameras clicking—next shot. Next shot. Next shot! I got familiar with the new routine, the early a.m. awakenings, the dressing room without a bathroom; I became a night pooper, and that started to seem normal. Or, if not normal, then just the way it was. A familiar distance wedged itself between me and Kel—a distance born of busyness, and impatience, and the occasional entitlement that comes from relapse. I remembered something Parker had said to me a long time ago, during my first show, when he was young. I was dressed to go out—some charity event, a fund-raiser for my foundation. Kel was coming with me. She was glittery; I was coiffed; the babysitter had arrived. "We're going to make money to take care of some sick kids," I told Parker. "Why," he said. "Why don't you just stay home and take care of us?"

Why indeed?

⁓

My four years away were perhaps at their core an acknowledgment of his question's validity—not an answer but a simple, humble nod. During my four years away from fame, the guilt had gone for a while, and so the blade had dulled. Now the guilt was back, and so were the sharp edges.

My children started to seem further away. What working parent has not had this experience—hearing what a child says but failing to actually listen? Or the experience of brushing your girl's straw-blond hair without once considering its color, or the way it pours over your palms.

My art began to feel dry to me, my yellows muddied. I wondered: How could we make *The View* better? What would the ratings tomorrow be? I watched those ratings go up, and I watched the trees turn colors, and I saw the real yellow was there, in the season and out of reach. Viv, my youngest, brought a leaf in from the yard. It was perfect, saffron and see-through, the veins raised in delicate ridges, the stem cool and pale.

And I dreamt. I dreamt deeply but without serenity or rest. I dreamt long lists of dry facts: DOBs and DODs and IFBs and ABCs. Sometimes Elisabeth was in my dreams, but I could never remember how, or where, or why. I'd get that feeling, though, that weird inner tug you get when you see someone or something and suddenly recall a fragment of a dream from the night before, or the year before; who knows when? She was in a crosswalk, or saying her times tables, 9x2, 5x3. Even in my dreams she stayed inside the lines. What would she think if she knew who I really was, if she knew the plain mundane facts of my mundane life that is nevertheless probably so different from hers: tummy mummies, Aunt Minnie, Chelsea's silver keys, the waffle house. Yes, no question we were different, but even in this strong brittle girl I saw something.

I invited her to my house that first fall of my being on *The View*, as the ratings were going up and my private life was coming down; I asked her to come over. And she did. And it was one of those beautiful blue September days when she showed up with her handsome football husband and perfect porcelain baby, and what I saw in her face was something like shock. Here was my house, pretty, pale yellow, with a tasteful round window made of stained glass, and four well-kept children who know their manners and have respect. Elisabeth came over and saw me in my suburban kitchen, and on my suburban deck. She saw that my daughter Chelsea has two blond braids, and my other daughter, Vivi, wears her hair in a close neat cap. She saw my boys play with Nick, a pooch so fat and friendly that he drags his nubbed tongue across your palm giving kisses. Elisabeth saw our family. I can't recall a thing we said when her family visited ours. Except this. "Your children are so *well behaved*." I had impressed her as a mother. This was a connection—for sure.

Elisabeth Hasselbeck was the captain and MVP of her division one softball team at Boston College. Who gets to be captain of a softball team as good as the one she was on in college? It's the rare woman, that's who. You have to be a leader. You have to want to win. Show me that girl. That's what I was saying to Elisabeth right from the start. Put down your IFB and pitch me a curve like I know you can. Stop with your sound bites and your predigested politics and think on your own two feet. I said to her, "You should throw a ball from the top of the set all the way across at the targets to win prizes for the audience." Imagine that. What a segment that would be. In some weird way, I figured *The View* would be successful if I could just get Elisabeth to throw that damned ball.

Set it fly. There it goes. Look up. It's padded, white, sutured with stitches; fat but still aloft, the ball arcs through the air, on the air, above the audience.

Waiting, watching—confetti! I asked for a monthly "Hasselbeck Hurl" to show her off, to remind her of herself.

It never happened.

I don't know why.

Blog 9/23/06

i hate rainy days
i would not survive seattle
gloom descends
necessary

it feels like a job
not my whole life
gratitude
earned

again . . . the press screams
my name in bold
skip good or bad
distraction

a gay one showed up
surrogate perfect girls in photos

from long island
my age 2

no matter how much i opened
he could not see in
took the easy way out
gay flag and all

jim mcgreeveys hands were shaking
in the green room
humanity trumps celebrity
grace enters for all

quitting aol
as my face appears
way 2 often
with a survey underneath

believe what u feel
u know
inside
what is real

CHAPTER 8

Talking about Barbra

Q&A with Rosie O'Donnell, Producer Jen Le Beau, and Interviewer Lauren Slater

ROSIE: Streisand is a direct connection to the light. She transmits on a frequency that comes in very clearly to nearly all of the population that samples her. Her channel comes in true and strong. She was broadband at a time when most people were dial-up.

LAUREN: And your mom loved Barbra Streisand?

R: Completely.

L: What would your mom think of you, if she were alive, and could see all that you have become?

R: I wonder about that. I think about it. If my mother had lived, I don't think I would have been able to accomplish all that I have.

L: Why?

R: I don't know. I do know that in many ways I am a child of Streisand's. I mean, she's only twenty years older than me. She was born April 24, 1942. I was born in 1962. My generation, we were all raised on her. Metaphorically we were nursed on her music, her essence and her individuality. She was the role model and an inspiration, a once-in-lifetime talent.

L: So what did you actually *do* to make this documentary?

R: The film is a tribute to her. It's a long love letter. It's a gift to her about the effect she's had on the culture and consciousness of so many people . . . My producer, Jen Le Beau, and I got into a car with our equipment and drove to Philly for opening night. Jen rigged the SUV with cameras. And we drove down.

JEN: On the way down we had a little movie marathon. We watched *A Star Is Born*.

R: We sat in the front row with her husband, Jim Brolan, and Donna Karan—

J: We were in the family section.

R: And the music started, the orchestra, the "Funny Girl" overture began. Barbra came out.

J: And Barbra's first words were "Rosie, I think I hear you." Ro and I looked at each other and her face went white.

R: What I felt, impossible to say.

J: And then Barbra sang "Funny Girl." When she was done she looked down at Rosie and said, "I think that was for you." And Ro burst into tears. It was truly incredible.

L: And did you guys go backstage after the show?

R: I decided not to go backstage at this point. I needed time.

L: So what happened?

R: We went home. I had a show in the a.m.

J: The ride back, from Philly to New York, was great. We talked. Ro kept saying, "So this is the part in the movie where the copter crashes and the music swells. Because real life can't be this good. Something bad is going to happen to me now."

L: I don't get it.

R: I can't help but feel I must be dying. Because I've gotten so much, been so lucky. If my life were an actual movie, it would be too, too flat almost, too *much*. I mean, my life is in some ways a story about a girl whose dreams *came true*. Because I spent my whole childhood dreaming of fame, of meeting Barbra, of being on Broadway, and it *all happened*. How weird is that? If my life were a screenplay, it would be a flop. The author would have to remedy the problem of too-muchness, of pure comedy, by inserting some tragedy to balance it all out. So here I am, just waiting for the tragedy to hit. If I were a screenwriter authoring my own life, the story would be this: girl from Rhonda Lane dreams of fame, dreams of Streisand, grows up, gets fame, gets Streisand, goes to Streisand concert, sits in front row, Streisand personally addresses her, the climax comes, and then—something tragic's gotta happen or the movie will fall flat—so then the girl from Rhonda Lane gets some incurable disease and is gone. This would have to be the ending of the screenplay.

On a less dramatic level, I wonder. I always wonder: *am I worthy? Why am I in the company of people like this?*

L: It's a dream come true, and that can be scary, in a knock-on-wood sort of way.

R: Yeah. Exactly. There's a moment in your mind where you're just like, "What the hell." But the strange thing is, even when all your dreams come true, you can keep making more.

L: So what are your dreams now?

R: In my dream version, we'd finish the film, and then I'd fly out to L.A. I'd drive to her house and

I'd sit down and I'd bring her the chocolate cake that she loves from the bakery in Brooklyn, and we'd sit down and watch the film and she'd think it was fantastic. But that's a dream. And it's a ways away. Right now we have a lot of very good raw material, but it's still being shaped.

L: Has she seen any of it?

J: Just a six-minute trailer. But she liked it!

R: Right. And that's huge. Because first there was a question of whether or not she would even allow us to do this documentary, this tribute, and then she did allow us. And then there was the question of whether she would watch it. And she did. I didn't go backstage after Philly, but I did go backstage after the New York City concert. And I handed her team the disc.

J: And then we waited.

R: Nerve-racking.

J: Very.

R: And finally, some time after Philly, we got the call. The call from her manager, Marty, who said she'd seen the footage on the plane, and loved it, and it was a go. October 24.

J: We thought it would be fun to get to Chicago real quick. So right after *The View* ended, on October 8, we flew down. We set up a tailgate party. We wanted to know what people say, and think, and feel, and do, when they hang out before a Streisand concert. So we put a button on Ro's blog: "Send us an e-mail and tell us if you're going to the concert and what Streisand means to you." From these e-mails we picked eighty-five or so people, and organized a party at a little restaurant around the corner from the concert. The party was a blast. Really special people there. We had a barbecue.

R: And then we went to the concert. When we went down to Philly, I had just started *The View*, and we went down, just me and Jen in our car. But Chicago happened in November. By then I'd been on air for well over a month. It was a whole different experience.

J: The difference in the experience between Philly and Chicago really shows how celebrity-ness changes your life. The Philly show was September 28 and we could go and be noticed but not overwhelmed. At the Chicago show, we couldn't even get down the aisle of the concert hall; it took us so long, because people were reaching out, trying to shake hands, get autographs, it took twenty minutes to move forward a foot.

R: But what was more stunning was to see Oprah come in, at the New York City show. One of the security guards said, "Winfrey'll be here in ten minutes."

You could hear the buzz of Oprah coming in.

There was a rumble. You could feel it. It was an intense energy, something building to a pressure point, very intense, and I was thinking, "Whoa!" I stood up with Kelli and Georgette and Charles, and I was clapping like everyone else watching her come and she came right down. I was two rows behind her. I said, "Excuse me, Ms. Winfrey. I'm a very big fan of yours." She shook my hand and looked at me and then gave me a hug the way she does. It is odd to watch Oprah hug, because she's not a good hugger, she is more of a lean-in-and-pat kinda hugger. I am the grab-and-hold-on kinda hugger . . . Yeah, it was really surreal and the audience was clapping and it was wild, it was wild, the whole thing.

L: I hate to admit this but I'm still not sure I really get what it is about Streisand, why she means so much to you. Honestly, what makes this story interesting to me is not Streisand, but how much you love her.

R: All people want to do is connect, right? And so many of us have been able to connect to ourselves, and to each other, through her. She's like a huge power outlet with millions of plug openings and millions of people have plugged into her, and are therefore able to shine on their own.

L: Well, I don't feel that way about Streisand at all. To me, she's, I don't know. She has not been a big part of my life at all. I mean, do you honestly think she's, as a talent, that she's heads and tails above Elvis? Or the Beatles? Here's the thing. The Beatles, what made them great is that they pushed the envelope. They pushed conventional music to its limits and in doing so defined a new genre, basically. They made rock 'n' roll. I don't see Streisand being that kind of innovator, and that's what I need in order to admire someone to the degree that you do.

R: She is an innovator. But if I have to explain it to you, then you simply can't see it.

L: Try.

R: No. That's like trying to explain why chocolate tastes good. You either get it or you don't, Slater. You don't have Babs's plug. You're not set to receive her signal.

L: Well, what is her talent, exactly? What is it that she does that's so extraordinary?

R: Singing. And the oddest thing is, she doesn't like to sing. She never wanted to be a singer. And twenty-seven years ago, she went onstage in Central Park, and she forgot the words to a song, and she was so horrified that she didn't perform live onstage again. She had massive stage fright, for twenty-seven years. This is a woman with the best voice in the world. And in 2000, when I saw her perform, I realized she actually used a teleprompter and refuses to go without one. And I thought, "God, if I were her friend, I would encourage her to do it without a net." Because we love her so, the audience would catch her if she fell.

L: So Streisand uses a teleprompter, which is not an IFB, but along the same lines, and it bothers you to no end that Barbara Walters relies on such props, and you say it makes Walters inauthentic, but when Streisand does it it's okay?

R: Here's the thing. When someone is really, truly genuine, it doesn't matter, the props don't matter. Streisand is genuine and it comes through. Even her anxiety comes through; she doesn't try to hide it. Walters uses the IFB to hide behind; she uses it in part in the hopes that it will make her appear smoother than she is. Streisand uses these props the way someone might use a crutch, or have a cast. It's obvious these things are there. It's obvious they need them. You can see it. I don't object to the props, or the technology or whatever. I object when they are used inauthentically.

For instance, in the recent Streisand concerts, I could tell, probably everyone could tell, she was nervous. She didn't try to hide who she was or what she was experiencing. And the remarkable thing was that I, and the audience, witnessed the growth of her confidence from the first concert to the last. By the end, she was having fun. She was relaxing. She was improvising. It was phenomenal for me to watch her acceptance of herself as a person. It was phenomenal to witness this transformation.

J: The whole tour in some ways was about transformation. Because during the Chicago concert we found out the Democrats were sweeping.

R: There were a lot of things changing then. Maybe the biggest thing for me, personally, was having Streisand stay at my house. I was always extremely nervous around Streisand until she stayed at my house in Miami. She was flying to Florida with her crew and something fell through with their hotel. So they called Kendall, my assistant. This is how it works in celebrity-ville. Somebody called Kendall because they knew I had a house, and it was an emergency and they needed it right away.

And Kendall came to me. She said, "You're not gonna believe this." I'm like, "What?" She said, "No, seriously, sit down. Streisand's people just called from the plane, they're en route to Miami, their hotel room fell through, and they want to stay at your house." I said, "Good God

Almighty, Kendall! Call them back and say yes immediately!" She said, "I already did."

And so Streisand slept at my house in Miami for a week while I did not sleep at my house in Nyack. Because I was just, it was just too much for me, in a great way. I could not, no way, fall asleep that night. Kelli kept telling me to go to sleep, but I didn't sleep the whole time she was there. I was always wondering, "Where is she right now?" And then she actually called me, in our New York apartment.

L: So you're in your apartment in the city for the night and you pick up the phone and it's Streisand?

R: I think Kelli picked up the phone. I'm not sure. I think Kelli answered it and she whispered, "It's Barbra Streisand!" I've talked to her before on the phone. But this time she was calling me to thank me about the house. Before this, I was to her just a fan who loved her, who said nice things about her, who sent her flowers a lot, constantly, who wrote her letters of inspiration. I'm sure in some part of her mind she's been like, "Oy vey."

But then when she came and used my house, she saw that I had a whole life there. She saw that I had children, and a craft room. She saw that I have a *Funny Girl* poster in my hallway, but she also saw that I was more than a crazed, obsessed fan. She saw me as a mother and a sister and an equal and all those things that you hope for. She painted me a picture in my craft room, and it was absolutely adorable. And she left me notes all over my house. "Sleep well. Sweet dreams." She is what I dreamed show business would be, and for those few days, that's also what it was.

J: And now you know, Ro, how your fans feel about you.

R: Yes, I do. And that's a startling thing to have to deal with. And this year is in part about coming to an acceptance of that, and taking responsibility for that, understanding that I am a satellite dish, smaller than Barbra but still a dish, and I have been given this job. I have been given the task of transmitting signals to people, and I have to hope my signals are clear and good.

But the bottom line right now: it is startling to realize that what I feel for Barbra is likely what others feel for me. And the question then becomes not only a who but a what. The questions are who am I and what does it mean to be real and also what will I do with my power?

L: What do you think you will do with it?

R: That's a question I have for myself. I have not answered it yet. I am first learning how to deal with the responsibility that comes from being what I am. Last time around, I'm not sure I knew so clearly that I was a transmitter. Now that I have understood this, I am also understanding that I need to develop some kind of spiritual practice, in part just to keep the chaos at bay, and to not get re-addicted. Barbra was a part of this.

L: How so?

R: Barbra is my best self. My ideal. Part of a spiritual practice may be to develop an ideal, which is not necessarily the same as idolizing. Idolization can be blind, but it can also be an expression of your highest hopes for yourself, and a reminder of what you need to strive for. After Barbra's tour was finished, I flew back to Nyack on the plane. And I was crying. Why was I crying? I was exhausted—doing *The View*, being a wife and mother, all at the same time. I was moved, emotionally. I kept thinking of her seeing my things, my life, the real Roseann O'Donnell, and the world felt less lonely. I used to love hide-and-seek as a kid. The thrill of finding a secret niche while someone counted to ten, waiting, crouched really low down. I was always so good at that game. I developed the strategy of hiding in plain sight, and it was amazing how hard it was for someone to find you when you were right in their line of vision. And I remembered how odd it was for someone to look straight past you, to literally not register you. It's the same creepy feeling I get when I go into a restroom and use the automated sensor-driven soap dispensers. Sometimes, for me, those dispensers don't work. It's like I'm not there. And then I am. The soap spurts out. Or the person suddenly realizes there's another person in their path, and you are caught. You are got. On the plane, flying back, that's what I felt. I felt sensed. I felt seen. I felt that this, perhaps, was what I needed to do for those who come to me—simply see them. Simply say, "I found you in your hiding place. You can come out now. Game's over."

And maybe they will. I will hold out my hand and do the best I can.

CHAPTER 9

The Sound of Color

I paint. I started after 9/11, started numbly, mindlessly, driven toward the canvas, toward whiteness I could cover with color. And since then, I have not stopped. Every aspect of painting pleases me, so much so that I want to do it at times over and above anything else. In my craft room I have tubes of Grumbacher oils, of Sennelier pastels, those bound wax sticks that, once pressed to the paper, leave behind a pure path of blue, or yellow. Saying it now, I can feel the color in my throat, behind my eyes, and sometimes at night, before falling asleep, I close my eyes and see the paintings I am not good enough to make—unfair, I can see them so well—the cobalt curls, the cadmium shapes blocked out and perfect. What actually is color? I could look up the explanation for that. But my question is more

120

of the metaphysical sort. Animals don't see color like we do. Their spectrum is narrower, and they get just these washed-out reds and muddy greens. So maybe, on some other planet, or even among us now, there are beings who can see beyond the spectrum. Maybe we are surrounded by indigos that are more vibrant than we can imagine, or reds that transcend red and are something altogether . . . what? Redder. Something. More.

I don't need anything more beautiful than what I have now. What is color? I can answer that question for myself. Color, I believe, is God's way of laughing, the liquid sauce in which he marinated his monochromic creations after he was finished. I imagine the first draft of our world was black and white, and God stepped away from his canvas, scratched his stubbly chin, and thought, "Hmmmm." He adjusted his beret and took a sip of the merlot he always kept by his easel. Something wasn't right about the mere mortals he'd sketched out. The faces were flat. The shadows looked like soot. The oceans were too tarry. What was it? He didn't know. He drew a rainbow, black and white stripes, that, when he sighed with disappointment, suddenly leaped into light, into yellow, into violet—some shadows—and in a snap the world was alive. It was Oz, and, thus inspired, he went on to make Roy G. Biv, the acronym every child learns in school, but they don't teach you it is much more. The spectrum is the original miracle, the pulse of our planet; it is fractal, fractured, illuminating. It is an utter refusal of flatness.

The Twin Towers had been flattened and the air smelled of smoke. I went to my craft room and squeezed some cadmium yellow onto my canvas. I remember that I was using Winton acrylic paint, pure pigment, devoid of the fillers that cheaper brands use. The paint glopped on and settled. It was thick, almost gelatinous. For a second I was scared. I had not painted in forty years, and as a kid I'd done it mostly out of art class obligation, the stick figures and square houses topped with a triangle.

I lowered the brush and then plunged in. I stroked outward, sudden swimmer, and I could feel the creaminess come right up to my wrists, and the sensation, it is difficult to describe what it feels like to push paint around, how it glides despite the roughness of the canvas, glides but does not melt, as water would, how a stroke starts in a puddle of color and radiates outward to end in a faint spray.

And so it was I started to paint. I had no knowledge, and no fear. All around me there was fear, and just seconds ago there had been fear inside me as well, but as soon as I started to push the paint fear left me and I was Roy G. Biv. I was not Rosie, not Ro, not Roseann, I was the brush plump with madder rose; and each shape I made became, in mere minutes, an object recognizable to me, a flower, a tree, a face, a frown.

Hello, world. I can control you. I can create you. Color is definite. It does not die.

⌖

The sky can look like a painting. I was on the plane coming back from the last Streisand concert, and when I looked out the window I thought of that first time, the smell of smoke that saturated the air for days after the attack, the Twin Towers falling, how quickly they crumpled. I looked at the sky, its tinges and the Rorschach shapes of the clouds, and I was in my craft room all over again, 9/12/01, making my canvases. And at the same time, in my mind, the sound of Streisand kept coming at me, and it felt as though sound could be chromatic, the red screech of someone's scream, or the yellow droplets of light laughter. For a moment sound and color merged, and I was overwhelmed. I was exhausted, exhilarated. I started to cry.

Streisand is an artist of unusual caliber, but there's more to it than that. The *more* is that she has also controlled her career in a way I want to emulate. Streisand has never allowed anyone to tell her what to do, how to proceed, when to stop, or start. She stopped singing for years and years, despite the pressure from the public and God knows whoever else. She directed movies she was advised not to; she played roles that were "wrong" for her. She heard what she needed to hear, and disregarded the rest. Above all, she has never ceded creative control to anybody else. The result. Her career has been orchestrated by her.

A life lived with integrity.

❧

I had come to understand that the show was not produced in the spirit of art, or even adventure. It lacked a heartbeat. A pulse. Humanity—truth. It lacked a mother's touch. Perhaps that was because it is run by a man. A man who had a different idea about what made good TV. Could I do *The View*—without being in charge—could I do just enough to get by—to not be embarrassed?

❧

Not now though. I was on fire, in color. And there, on the plane, I thought of something Streisand had told me. Early in her career, she had explained to me, she'd had a hard time accepting her talent and the tremendous power it had over people. Sometimes her talent had even felt like a curse. But now, at sixty-four, now for the first time she said she was starting to feel some acceptance of what she could do, and the responsibility that comes with it. Now, she can love that she is loved, and by so many. I think that means Streisand is coming to see her own spectrum, and finally understanding how much joy her rainbow brings to people. I would say she is starting to see she has the power, the sheer wattage, to illuminate very deeply into our collective night.

Ruthie, my Kabbalah teacher, tells me I am a leader, whether I like it or not. She says in my next life I will probably come back as a dog, certainly as someone or thing with no ability to have an effect, but in this life I am a leader. I have no choice—it is my *tikkun*, a word that means many things in Hebrew, "transformation," or, in terms of the Kabbalah, "the reconciliation of two seemingly opposite things," like the desire for fame and anonymity at the same time, the desire to be visible and invisible, to be a part of a community and also to be alone.

"You can't stay in the craft room your whole life, Rosie," Ruthie once told me. She is right. I *am* a leader, and sometimes I like it and sometimes I don't. I have a spectrum; I believe everybody does, but for reasons I will never understand, people are influenced by mine, and so I should not compromise it. Ever. This is what I saw on the plane, going home. I was a part of *The View* and *The View* was a part of me, for at least as long as my contract lasted. I needed to try and make it a better show.

I love the landing of planes. I am always happy to touch down. I saw the city appear, its frail lines coming clearer, a photograph in fluid, the landscape beneath evolving from little to life size as we approached the runway. No matter how many times I have flown, I always find it odd to see the world from up high, to see it as a toy town, a Monopoly game board, and to watch as it slowly assumes its real dimensions.

I have also learned, however, that even things you find indisputably real, or obvious, are not necessarily so. Coming down from on high, I saw the Empire State Building as a silver sword, and the George Washington Bridge strung with little lights. How can one argue with facts such as these—the existence of a building, or a certain stream of light? Some facts, you think, are inarguable. But even this is not so.

For instance, 9/11. I remember 9/11 crisply, as most New Yorkers do. And I have written what I recall of it in this book, some chapters ago. I showed my brother Eddie what I had set down here, and he got upset. "What?" I asked him. "What's wrong?"

"Don't you remember what really happened on 9/11?" he asked. "You have not written it correctly."

"What do you mean?" I said.

"Don't you remember me calling you? We were both at NBC." (Eddie used to work at NBC, a few floors above where I produced *The Rosie O'Donnell Show*.)

I said, "I remember speaking to you on 9/11."

He said, "On 9/11, I called you and said, 'What are you doing?' And you said, 'What are you talking about?' and I said, 'We're under attack. We have to leave the building.' And you said, 'No, Eddie, I'm doing my show.' And I said, 'Roseann, you have to leave the building. We're under attack; you have to get out of the city. And get the kids . . .' And then you said to me, 'No, Eddie, I can't, I'm doing my show.'"

Now, I have no memory of the events Eddie is describing and I have no way of finding out whether they are true or not, and it is in some ways besides the point. I'm less interested in that and far more interested in the fact that such discrepancies can occur in the first place. Here we are, two solid, reasonably sane people, and we have two entirely different accounts of the same event. Maybe he's remembering it the way he is because he has some need to see himself as my big brother, some sort of savior. Or maybe my failure to remember the situation as it was has to do with my inability to accept my vulnerability. I honestly don't know.

As it turns out, 9/11 is not the only disagreement my brother and I have about reality. He and I had one of the biggest fights of our life when I said in an interview that I never went to my mother's funeral. And he was livid. And he called me up, it was years ago, and he said, "You were at Mommy's funeral, I sat next to you." I said, "Eddie, I was not. Daddy took me and Maureen to the wake in the back of the blue station wagon, we saw her dead body, everyone started to scream, he took us out the side entrance, put us back in the car, had a panic attack on the way home, told us just to be quiet, made us go to our rooms, and then we were not allowed to go to the funeral." Eddie was adamant. We had a huge fight. I was sure I knew the truth, sure of what was real, and also, at the same time, I could barely hear a whisper inside me, and this whisper was shaped like a question mark. It is the whisper that makes the world feel always a little wobbly. It is learning to stand solidly while the whisper is whispering that constitutes strength. If you don't have the whisper, you are arrogant. If you have the whisper and are paralyzed because of how it clashes with what you think you know, you are neurotic. If you have the whisper and stand trembling—or not—despite the steady stream of small sound, you have some courage, better known as integrity. My life has been about going forward despite the curve of the question mark. I am certain I did not go to my mother's funeral.

My children go to a school that encourages creativity and common sense. Every child learns to play an instrument; every child learns to sew, to garden, to read, to write, to cook, to add, to subtract, and to sculpt. The school also emphasizes multiple intelligences, and encourages not only language literacy but visual literacy as well. I never learned how to draw, which is one reason why my painting will always be deficient. All the passion in the world cannot replace technique. My daughter Chelsea, on the other hand, can wield a pencil as easily as she wields a fork, and I love to watch her do this, the nimble lines she makes, and how from a seemingly disjointed jotting of slashes and dots, the hindquarters of a horse emerges, and then, look, a leg, a mane, a snout, with a blaze of black running down it. Chelsea draws what she loves, and what she loves are animals. You can feel her love in the soft way she sketches the ponies, and you can see her love in the way, every night, she takes Zoë, her Australian shepherd, to sleep on her bed with her.

While I can feel so much compassion for people it hurts, I am oddly deaf when it comes to a connection with nonhuman counterparts. Chelsea amazes me for many reasons; she is opaque to me, and beautiful, like stained glass you cannot see through, gorgeous glass whose color refracts back at you, and no matter how hard you stare, you cannot see through to the other side. I think Chelsea sees herself in animals, feels at home in their language-less kindness.

⌁

Early on at *The View* we did a show on pets. What is the best sort of pet for your family to have? There are dogs, cats, gerbils, guinea pigs. Is this interesting? Do

we care? Pick your battles, Ro. This is what I thought.
I had enough to do just trying to get them to change
their bland beige set into something bold and blue.
And besides, this year was supposed to be about learning to accept mediocrity, not always having to strive
for the stars.

No matter how many times it happens, I can never quite
comprehend it. The "it" are the controversies in which
I have, at various times, found myself embroiled. Here
and there the conflicts seem deserving of attention. But
more often than not, the hot water I find myself in is
truly tepid, but the press brings it to a boiling point.

After Danny DeVito came on, I made a comment
about how many people, worldwide, were talking about
his apparent inebriation. Because it struck me then and
it strikes me now. So I said, on *The View*, I said they were
talking about it in Turkey, in Kenya, in Lebanon; I said
people were talking about it in China and then I tried to
imitate a Chinese accent, which is what I try to do all the
time—imitate people, black or white, here or there. Capturing other voices and styles fascinates me. Sometimes,
when people speak, I cease listening to their words and
zoom in instead on the cadence, and it can seem lovely,
and at other times absurd, all this verbiage, these seem-

ingly random consonants clattering on the string that is sound. My use of the words *ching* and *chong* were meant largely to illuminate what can occasionally seem to me like random strings of sound.

I honestly did not intend to offend anyone, which is why I was surprised to learn that Barbara Walters was receiving phone calls, letters, and e-mails from top Asian community leaders. If I had to summarize their various points, it might come out as this: How can Rosie O'Donnell insult Asian people and act in a racist way when she posits herself as a champion of human rights, and so avidly works and speaks against prejudice, especially concerning gays?

My point is not to defend myself; my point is simply to say what it is I feel. I felt tired. I know I am not a racist and made that comment with no ill will. I come, as I wrote in the statement I later released, in peace. I tried to say so but it is hard, once the media machine gets going, to make your voice heard, even for a loudmouth like me. People pressed me to apologize.

I was now at the point, with the show and in my life, where I didn't have time to even paint, and painting is a necessity for me. I had no time to think through the whole episode, so I was therefore not ready to make an apology. Because before I apologize, I want to have some understanding of what it is I have done. This is essential for me. Apology without understanding is useless. Here was my dilemma. I could not reflect on the meaning of the events because my mind was perversely consumed with replaying the forbidden words.

I wound up apologizing not because anyone pressured me to, and not because I was slowly going crazy. I apologized because one person, a hairdresser, with a few simple words, broke the brain lock and let me understand. The hairdresser I am referring to is Asian. I have always liked to watch her work when given the chance. When I was a little kid, my mom would wash my hair, and it sometimes felt too rough, her fingers kneading my scalp as though she were willing it to rise; she worked the suds into my skin and then hosed out the lather, streams of water, sometimes scary, galling over my upturned face, that soap sting in my eyes.

This Asian woman though, when she washed people's hair she was so light in her touch, so precise and careful. Even her lather seemed contained and fragrant, and tiny bubbles seeded her hands. And one day, a week or so after the incident, while I was watching this Asian hairdresser, I asked her, "Were you offended?"

The hairdresser put her hands up in the air, like, *mensa mensa.*

"Seriously," I said. "Seriously, you were offended?"

"Yeah," she said. "When I was a little kid they used to say to me *ching chong chinaman*, and it was very derogatory, and it did sort of hurt my feelings a little bit when you said that."

And suddenly, *zap!* No amount of scolding or demanding or even rightful raging did it. What did it for me was one woman's simple truth, told person to person. Me to you. Understood. I'm truly sorry.

"Okay," I said. "I'm apologizing!"

And so I apologized. I called my publicist and issued a statement. "Listen," I said. "I never meant to hurt anyone's feelings. But if even one person who knows me took it that way, then it's not okay. That was never the intent of the joke, but if someone took it that way then I would want to correct it." I also said something else that looking back on it I see undercut the apology a little bit, something to the effect of "this is just the way my mind works and I may do it again."

Now why did I say that? Some lingering feeling of resentment I suppose, resentment over feeling so profoundly misunderstood. Now, in retrospect, I wish I had been a bit more pure in my public apology, because that's what I expect of myself—purity, or at least the intent. I want for myself a near perfect performance, a voice, a song, a self in precisely the right key.

⌀

There was a snowstorm. It started out soft and fluffy, for about two seconds, and then a warm wind blew in and the flakes turned to needles of ice, they came clattering down on the world and by midnight the trees were glass. People were saying, "Well, maybe after all we will have a white Christmas," and Manhattan was lit up the way it always is, lights and wreaths swinging from wires. There were Salvation Army people ringing their bells and motorized dwarfs bowing in bay windows. Barbara Walters was planning on going away for vacation, and there was quite a lot of talk about what to get the staff for gifts. I wanted to suggest to Joy and Elisabeth that while Barbara was away, they go without their IFBs. That could be their gift to me. In turn, I wanted to get the staff—every one of them—a neat present, unusual, some swerve.

❧

The kids were scrubbed, the book bags packed, and Chelsea came up to me, near tears. "I can't find Zoë," Chelsea said.

"I'm sure she'll make her way up to your bed whenever she is ready," I said. I looked up at her from the book I was reading and was struck, as I often am, by her loveliness. She was the one, of my four, whom I had the hardest time with as a baby, but she is now, of my four, the most gracious.

Chelsea looked concerned. "Zoë always comes when I call her," Chelsea said, and then, to demonstrate this fact, she called—"Zo-ëeee"—her hands cupped around her mouth. We waited for a moment, maybe two, and we could not hear the clicking of toenails that was the usual response.

Nick, our lemon yellow Lab, slept peacefully in a pool of lamplight. Both dogs wander outside, and although our property is gated, they always ran free.

"She'll be back," I reassured Chelsea.

Chelsea padded off in her slippers, slid open the glass doors leading to the deck, and peered out into the night. I stretched, heard the bones in my back crack. I looked at my daughter looking for her dog. It was 7:00 p.m., the dinner dishes stacked on the counter, Parker cross-legged on the floor, drawing with his Magic Markers. The light from the room made Chelsea's hair look more golden than it really was, and her form was lined with night, edged with inky black.

Something occurred to me then. I was here. I was busy, I was tired, I was overworked, but I was, indisputably, here at my home with my children, before bed, one of whom was looking for a lost dog. What could be more normal, and also more significant? When I was doing my own show, even these small but crucial family moments were totally lost to me; I was consumed. I rarely got home for dinner. Now, I was home almost every night, cranky, yes, but home.

When I had my own show, I could never call in sick, but sitting there, watching my daughter feel fear, it occurred to me I could call in sick tomorrow if I needed to; there were three people other than me holding this big ball.

"Mom," Chelsea said. "Zoë's lost."

I was starting to think she was right. Zoë is an anxious, obedient animal who comes when called, and who sticks close to familiar territory. I wondered if Nick, the Lab, had led her out beyond the fence, and then not bothered to lead her back.

"Honey," I said. "She'll be fine. She's maybe down by the water."

Chelsea began to cry. "We need to find her!" she said.

I was tired; Kelli was in the city; it was me and four kids. The last thing I wanted to do was pile my brood into my car to drive around looking for a dog. I called Geraldine, our nanny, who came and took Chelsea and Parker out in the car while I stayed home with Viv and Blake. I put them to bed. I lay down next to Blake. There was a shadow on his wall, and it looked like the yin and yang symbol. The curve of darkness cupped in the curve of light. I've never known, or asked, what it stood for. It seemed, suddenly, that I knew. It meant you could be two in one. You could be both dark and light, good and bad, tethered and free, brilliant and not. I was striving for excellence on the set, but I could also not show up on that set if my kids were sick, if the dog died, on a bad day—if need be. I was a celebrity, but I was also a plain mom lying with her five-year-old in a bed, like millions of other tired mothers all across this country, right now. I fell asleep.

An hour or so later Geraldine brought Chelsea and Blake back. Zoë could not be found. Chelsea was devastated. She slept in my bed that night, my girl, and somewhere, hopefully not far from here, her dog was figuring out the maze she was in, slowly scenting her way home.

⌒

I had not slept well because Chelsea had not slept well; she had sobbed half the night, and kept getting up, tapping on the window, hoping to see some shadow of her dog. Jane Goodall. She had talked about the connection between people and animals. And Temple Grandin had recently written a book about animal minds, and how they share some similarities with the way autistic people think. Why not a show on, no, not pets, but on animals and what the bond between us and them is made of? Why not a show about how autistics share similar cognitive capacities with nonhuman species, or, for that matter, why not a show on autism itself? Or on foster care? Or on cults? Or on psychics? Or on depression? A whole one-hour show. Not a segment, but a whole devoted hour. The idea excited me.

You can't get breadth or depth in a seven-minute segment.

Whole-hour theme shows was not what *The View* had been about. I was not trying to take it over. That had honestly never been my intent. My intent was to make a show that would allow every single one of us with our particular talents to shine. My intent was to make a show that was excellent and that still allowed me to have a family.

I didn't know that *The View* would expand its views and allow whole-theme shows on autism, foster care, depression, shows that refueled me and that I loved. I didn't know how angry I would get at Barbara, nor how much capacity we both have for forgiveness. I didn't know that Zoë, Chelsea's nervous dog, had in fact *not* run away, that the whole time we'd been looking for her she'd been locked accidentally in the family van, where she'd been riding with us the day before, sleeping in the backseat, out of view. *The View.* I could never have guessed a single syllable could hold so many contradictions.

❧

I left that day with an inexplicable sense of hopefulness, excitement. I felt there were opportunities for me, yins and yangs, this's and that's, mother and worker, famous and anonymous, excellent and banal. Bill Geddie had intimated that my theme segments were very possible. I pulled into our driveway. Chelsea had been crying for almost twenty-four hours straight and still no sign of Zoë. The plan was to make Lost Dog signs and post them around town. Geraldine went to get a stack of papers from the family van. I could hear, from the kitchen, the door slide open, and then, in her lovely Irish accent, "Holy be Jesus," and an excited, exuberant overwhelming yapping—there was no doubt. That was Zoë!

We ran outside. Zoë was running in circles, trembling, jumping, peeing, pooping, rolling over, scuttering to a stop, running again; she was saved. Saved! Chelsea scooped the dog up in her arms, buried her nose in the mottled fur. We brought the now-freed Zoë a bowl of water. We could not believe we hadn't heard her bark through the windows. Maybe she had only barked for a while. Maybe, as hours passed, she'd given up hope, curled into a corner.

Much later on, toward evening, after everyone had calmed down, after Zoë had been debriefed and untraumatized and Chelsea had had time to comb the snarls and comfort her hound, I knelt down and cupped Zoë's bony chin in my hand. No one was around to see me. I'd never studied the dog up close. I saw, this close, that she had very pale whiskers sprouting from her snout, and that her eyes were the color of melted butter. "Zoë, Zoë," I said. And for the first time I felt a little love for the yappy, nervous dog. I felt grateful I'd been around to see her lost, and then found. I had *The View* to thank for that, for a schedule that was flexible enough to let me live a family life. Things were coming together. "Yes they are, Zoë," I said. I scratched her chest. And for a brief moment, I felt a kinship with this little beast, so different from me on the one hand, but so familiar on the other. You can see it in the eyes, the similarities. And at the same time, you can see it in the eyes, the differences. The bottom line difference is maybe this. Animals are indisputably and always themselves. They cannot lie. They cannot cheat. They cannot act. "Zoë, Zoë," I said. I stroked the small skull.

CHAPTER 10

Trumped

So, Donald. Donald Trump. I have in my home office, on my window ledge, several pieces of true Trump merchandise: Cologne, vodka, bobble head, each piece packaged in royal purple wrappings, gilded gold bows, bottles sprayed silver and embossed.

All throughout those trying Trump days, the merchandise reminded me that this was not a *man* who was spewing such ugliness—*my little fat Rosie can't wait 'til I sue the degenerate fat ugly third rate fatassfatlittlemyRosiedegenerateuglyfat* . . . he just kept going. I started to feel somewhat sorry for him. I also started to see that he was not a man. He had once maybe been a man, or a boy, but that human spirit seemed to have gotten lost to a mechanical repetitive meanness, a push-button person with its circuits askew. He'd been on the *Today* show with Meredith Viera during his rampage and she had said something like, "How about saying, right now on the *Today* show, 'I'm not gonna bring up Rosie again'?" And he sat there for about two seconds and then he was sucked straight back into this maniacal rant. I kept Trump products in my office because they reminded me that my "attacker" was not a human being but a windup toy with Tourette's, a man who had allowed himself to get pulled so deeply into capitalism that he had turned his entire being into a product with a price tag on it; he was gift wrapped and stuffed with Styrofoam.

But I'm ahead of myself here. I was in a good place when the Trump business began. Zoë was home. Streisand had stayed in my house and lovingly left pieces of herself behind. *The View* was beginning to open itself up to more and more of my suggestions, not just about the set, or the lighting, or how to usher the audience in; they were taking more risks, slowly, like children stepping into the sea. Joy and Elisabeth did not let go of their IFBs when Barbara left for her extended Christmas vacation, but I was able to be okay with that, able to respect them for knowing what they would and would not do. And I felt they would soon make the leap into spontaneity, soon, but not now; I could sense their loosening. The autism show had been approved; I was going to contact Temple Grandin, whom I had never met before, but it's opportunities such as these, meeting people such as her, that make my work worth it.

At home, we were getting ready for Christmas, the tree up, the lights laid out, and when it was over, we would go to Florida, and I would have a week away from the show, a week just to be with my kids, to catch up with them and their lives—essential. The night of December 19, Kel and I were relaxing, watching TV, and on came Trump in a press conference about his benevolence vis-à-vis Miss USA and her expected recovery from an alcohol problem. To say I found it distasteful would be an obvious understatement. I have a problem with the whole notion of Miss USA as it's defined and enacted by men like Donald, taking twenty-year-old girls, parading them around onstage in bikinis while he and a bunch of other old men give them a score, and if they win—then what? They become Donald's own doll for a year, his brand for 365 days, because he'd bought the pageant, which means, to me at least, he'd bought the girls, and buying people, especially young nubile ones who probably make you far more money that you pay them to do your bidding— of course I have a problem with this. It's like watching a pimp and a prostitute. And we're all participating in it.

So I was not pleased to find Trump on the TV screen in my bedroom, holding his press conference in which he stood there with a twenty-one-year-old girl he believed had acted inappropriately, and then to see him announce, in an appropriately trumped-up voice full of trumped-up compassion, that he would "give her a second chance," or some such thing. He would allow her to keep the crown, his tone full of righteousness and factory-made feeling, the whole thing designed to convey to the public the impression he had carefully crafted. It is Trump's falseness that angers me more than anything. Call it like it is. That's all I ask. Don't pretend. If you fake life, then you have damaged the social and biological fabric on which we all depend, for breath and love.

I certainly hadn't been planning on imitating him on TV; he wasn't written into the segment, but he'd been on my mind since I'd seen him the night before, and so when something in the conversation that day on *The View* reminded me, I brought him up. I spoke my mind. People found it funny. I said he had gone bankrupt twice; in fact, some of his companies had filed for bankruptcies.

To him I guess it felt like I was saying he had a communicable disease with a bad odor. He took the bankruptcy comment hard, very hard. I honestly did not anticipate the malice of his response; but looking back at it, I can understand it. I assumed Donald believed he had money. I did not assume Donald believed he *was* money. But apparently he does. The violence of his response suggests to me that money is the means by which he has defined himself, so the bankrupt statement felt devastating to him, and his coins came clattering down. The stuffing of his self spilled out—think of a torn scarecrow, only instead of hay, it's crisp $100s blowing through the cornfields, spiraling up into the sky. Money was blowing everywhere; he burst open like a birthday piñata and coins came out, and instead of getting to work repairing the rip, he kept spilling and spilling until he was thigh-high in cold cash, gold coins, and rage. On my end, I watched. I caught some of the coins he threw my way. I looked at them, ran my finger round their rim. Interesting, I thought. Very interesting.

It had been, so far, an abnormally warm December, the warmest since people had begun keeping records in 1852. On Trump day, the weather was fifty-two degrees, and the lilacs were beginning to bud, as were the rhododendrons, their sealed pods loosening at the seams, ruffled bits of pink petals visible. The children loved it—they could play outside without a jacket or a hat, but if you read the newspaper closely and completely you could find the articles that commented on this strange situation, and if you went to certain Web sites you could see, with the aid of visual graphs, the upward spiking trend, or the polar ice caps then and now, the *then* showing large opaque sheets, the circle of ice radiating far afield, and the *now,* the ice diminished, wedges of lime green land showing, chunks of melting ice atop which polar bears precariously balanced.

I was in my craft room looking at polar bear pictures, wondering about the ominous warmth, on Trump day. The world was warming up faster, it seemed, than anyone had predicted, and I was surfing the Web, and I came to a sight that showed polar bears. The text explained the warming, melting ice left them in a strange land where they were slowly starving. I saw one photograph of a bedraggled white bear, his once fluffed fur now matted, and the hull-shaped rib cage showing through, and my own ribs hurt, down deep.

I was looking closely at the pixilated image, so at first I didn't hear Kel come in. Then I turned. She stood at the entrance to the room, the door open, so behind her I could see the tips of trees, the branches bare and black, the plump buds a sci-fi green. "They will probably want to talk to you," Kelli said.

"Who will?" I asked.

"ABC," she said. "The Trump crap."

She was right, of course. I had learned by now what ABC wants and doesn't want me to say or do. Probably they would want me to apologize to Trump. I wasn't going to. I didn't say anything slanderous or libelous. And this is the job they were paying me to do. I was doing it the best that I could, and I couldn't do my job if they were going to want me to apologize all the time.

There's the rub, as Hamlet once said. *The View*'s relationship to me was one of fundamental contradiction. They had hired me, and continued to want me on the show, because I had brought them from a faltering position to a top-rated talk show that was attracting new viewers weekly. Great. Great! But they were also constantly trying to tone me down, which made no sense. A toned-down me, a washed-out, Xeroxed version of Rosie O'Donnell would not work. I am successful because I am who I am, this range of color undiluted.

Trump was their problem, not mine. I told Kelli that, we talked a while, and then she left. I shut down the computer and started to paint, the music cranked up high. I knew what they would do next. I, for my part, was going to do yellow and blue, but I guessed they would call Barbara where she was vacationing on a yacht in the middle of some exotic sea. I pictured it now like moving marble, the boat chiseled from a chunk of pure gold. I pictured her with white-gloved waiters. She was off in the rich people's club. As it turns out, Donald is a member of that club.

Now, allow me to digress, for just a moment. Like I said, the issue of money and clubs has been a fraught one for Barbara and me this year. To me, she is clearly rich in a way that I am not and never will be, but when I said this on air, she practically turned the color of cranberry and shot me one of her steely stares. What had I said that so shocked her? I had said that she was wealthier than I, and she had responded as though I had slapped her. I find money fascinating, how full of shame and secrecy it is. Why is money so private? Why, when I talk about money out loud, as I often do, is it perceived by so many as crass? Kelli says that it sounds like I'm bragging when I say "I have more money than a human needs," but because in my mind money is not really linked to worth, it's a simple statement of fact.

However, let me double back on myself, because what I've just said is not totally true. I've said that in my mind money is not linked to worth. If this were totally true for me, than I would not care whether I was offered a salary of $50,000, $150,000, or $150 million. But when I think about what I want to do next year, the money figures in. So am I not being honest here?

The money figures in because I have, like every other American, a tiny whisper of fear that the bottom might fall out, but it's so tiny as to be almost imperceptible. What really makes the money figure in for me is that I know it's a reflection of how the other person sees me. Even if I don't measure by money, the people hiring me sure as hell do, so if someone offers me a low salary, it feels like a blow, because the translation is simple: you suck. What I can say for sure is that if everyone agreed to separate money from worth, if money were truly *just money* and had no symbolic meaning beyond itself, then I am at a point in my life where I neither want nor need more.

I talk about these things. I don't understand why

you are not supposed to talk about these things. So when I brought it up that day on *The View*, Barbara looked ill. What I was trying to discuss: that it isn't the amount of money necessarily that makes someone rich; there are other intangibles. I might have more money than Barbara. I don't know, but even if at some point I did, she will always be richer than me. She's part of high society, a club I cannot ever be admitted to. And when I visit her club, like the time I went to her home for dinner, it is, for me, like visiting another planet. Barbara Walters could lose all her money and she will still be high society, and I could make six times the money I have, and I will always be a working-class kid. I find this fascinating.

And for this reason I find Donald fascinating.

When he cracked, Barbara was on vacation, in the ocean, and ABC obviously called her and told her about the "problem." Before this happened I did not fully appreciate how much Donald is a member of the rich persons' club. I knew it, but I hadn't given it much thought. In any case, Barbara wrote a message for the press; I picture her leaning against the silver railing of the ship, her blond hair blowing in the wind, a pen poised above pressed stationery paper, penning her missive like a 1940s film character. She is glamorous. Her message to the press was glamorous, in that it was carefully carved, artfully phrased, because Barbara's deepest wish in life, it sometimes seems, is for everyone to just get along. On the one hand she has Grace Kelly glamour, but the next moment, flip a switch, she's a tired grandmother trying to rein in a family feud.

"Both Rosie and Donald are high-spirited, opinionated people," she stated, or some such thing. "Donald has been a friend of *The View* for many years," and separately she stated that "I do not regret for one moment my choice to hire Rosie," etc., etc. ad infinitum. The message was short but clear. No chaos, please. Like my nana at the Thanksgiving table. She just wants peace. She's perfectly happy to be the matriarch of the family and make sure the children don't fight. And we're all the children.

It may be that this is one of the few times Barbara failed to finesse a situation. Donald was not, apparently, appeased by her remarks. What happened next proves that nastiness can be pure, a paradox indeed. Pure nastiness.

He went on seemingly every show, spoke to every media outlet that he could. He groaned in a strange way, almost salivating over the words: "I look forward to taking lots of money from my nice fat little Rosie." Totally creepy. He was sadistic in a deeply disturbing way, and I watched him from afar. It was like seeing a specimen squirming on a slide in high school science class, hmmm. Poke here and it lashes its tail. Add this salt to the brine and it shrivels up. Donald, for some reason, also reminded me a lot of the garden slugs we used to get on our front steps when we were kids. They'd come in the late spring, after rains, gelatinous, goopy slugs, some five inches long, sleek and wet, leaving sticky trails in their wake. The strangest thing about these slugs: if you sprinkled salt on them then— poof. It was like magic. They shriveled up so small and desiccated, they practically disappeared. I could write one small comment on my blog and Donald would predictably distend, flowing forth with a torrent of insults—*fatuglydegenerateslobfatass*—and then, in another second, he'd appear on some talk show looking wrinkled and old and empty, with a Jell-O orange comb-over.

The first day he was, perhaps, his crassest, because he commented on Kelli, how he'd like to take her. "Rosie's a bully," he said to some New York newspaper. "She's an extremely unattractive person who doesn't understand the truth . . . She has an extremely low aptitude," yadda yadda yadda. The strategic beauty and human sadness of remarks such as these is that they confirm in the attacker the very qualities the attacker is so desperately trying to ascribe to the other person. Thus, Trump went down, and down, and down.

The next day, I brought Kelli with me to *The View.* I said little about Donald except that I had Kelli with me because I didn't want her to leave me for a man with a comb-over. After the show was over we got right into the car, we were surrounded by reporters and microphones and clicking cameras. I rolled down the window and yelled, "Ho ho, Merry Christmas," and then, vavoom, we took off.

We went to visit Georgette Mosbacher. We brought her McDonald's because her dog had died and she was a wreck. She couldn't get out of bed. So we showed up with a huge bag of Mickey D's. I love Georgette because she loves her dogs, and her McDonald's fries. She'd already gotten a new puppy, and he was adorable, big floppy paws and more fuzz than fur. It is hard to articulate the love Georgette has for her dogs; it must be similar to what Chelsea feels, and thus her grief was just bottomless. We sat around, and played with the new puppy, and I held her, and she did all the perfect puppy things, which was exactly what I needed. We were in Georgette's apartment, in Georgette's grief, three women and a baby animal, and it felt, for a second, so serene, the Donalds of the world so far away. It was wonderful. I pulled the puppy up to my neck and felt her breathe against my skin. I closed my eyes. When I opened them again, everything was just as it was—real—an oasis made of milk shakes and love.

I made an effort not to watch TV. It was December, what, 22 or 23, the Trump debacle had barely begun, but already felt as if it had been happening for years, because he just droned on and on.

I did not anticipate, however, that he would be cruel enough to do what he did to Barbara. She should have been left alone.

◦

My friend Jackie came over that night. "Aren't you scared?" she kept asking me. "Ro, aren't you scared?"

Jackie comes from a family where the men were powerful, and frightening. When I left my show all those years ago, I realized the freedom that comes from not being famous. How fantastic, to be without a bodyguard. The privacy, the extension of space. The unself-consciousness. The expanded opportunities for reverie. You could leave your door propped open on a summer afternoon. Fantastic. You didn't need a sky-high gate and, as a result, you could see the sky. I reveled in it. And I swore I would never have as much security as I'd had when I was famous, whether I needed it or not. The price had been too high. In protecting my life, I had lost it.

That's the thing about fame. It is a dangerous game, because fame, the drug, can sneak up on you in increments. You don't notice the increments, that you're increasing the dosage until you're so far away from ever making eye contact with another human being and being "real," that you don't even know you're not "real" anymore.

So no, Jackie, I was not afraid. I was getting ready to go on vacation. I was decorating my tree. I was not wounded, or worried. However, what happened next changed everything.

～

Trump was everywhere. He said that he himself had spoken to Barbara, and Barbara herself had told him that she was not a fan of mine. That he should never get in the mud with pigs. He outed Barbara. A private conversation with him both outed her and probably twisted the truth of what she had said, on air. He dragged a seventy-seven-year-old woman, a living legend, into his fight; he's a sixty-something-year-old guy, I was a forty-five-year-old woman, and he had to go and drag a septugenarian into the fray, someone who, no matter what her strengths, is in some ways more vulnerable than he is. What a coward. I was thinking all these things. I was packing my bags for Florida. I felt a deep winter chill inside, despite the perversely warm weather. Trump announced he would probably sue me. Go ahead, big guy. The words of Barbara reformulated by Donald kept swinging at me, from the side, now the top, a punch here, now there, duck and cover. I was hurt now. I was wounded. And whatever comfort and appreciation I had started to feel vis-à-vis my place on *The View*, and my potential role in its production—gone. Up in smoke. Trump had wounded two women, and for what? As for me, the worst part of it was that I knew, from the get-go, twisted though he was, I knew in my heart that Barbara had said those things. In one way or another, she had betrayed me. Trumped, I was. Tired.

Blog 12/27/06, Miami

so what happens
when u say the emperor has no clothes
the comb over goes ballistic
via phone to mr king

choices
every minute
every day
everyone

i imagine it is interesting
as celeb feuds tend 2 b
so here r my thoughts

didnt watch
didnt u tube
restrict

i have no time 2 make art now
i am only off friday
which is never enuf
to detox

the pipes get full
bits of sludge
clog the flow

so tiny books
now
express in torn images
my inside

i was raised reading ms magazine
i remember the burning of bras
as women demanded equality
in unison

beauty pageants
where women were paraded around
judged valuable or not
by old white men

it is always old white men

they added a talent portion
and gave away college degrees
they evolved—beauty pageants
and eventually—nearly faded away
for good

remember the seventies

a young girl in nyc
meets a pimp
he cons her into a life of illusion
she works for him

no fun—no fucking—no future
she is owned
when she sneaks out
to party the night away
he freaks

he roughs her up a bit
shames her in front of the others
teaches her to behave
for his own benefit

and just when we lost all hope
cagney and lacey showed up

Rosie O'Donnell

they cuff the pimp
they free the girl

marybeth and christine
would never
be friends with a pimp

this is reality tv
like it or not
same same same
as vivi says

CHAPTER 11

Thank You for the Show

Florida. The state with the prettiest name. Star Island, where we live. My dream house, a reality now. Fragments of Streisand here and there, little notes she left for me, lying where she placed them. I smile whenever I see one. Miami is dazzling, the ocean emerald, a twinkle, as though whisked by some fairy's wand. Heaven, I imagine looks like this. Inside the house is bright, bleached and clean. The patio with its lounge chairs and the pool looks like an ad in a magazine. The pool is heavenly blue, so clear I could see the silver drain warbling way down by the bottom.

We jumped in. We hugged our knees to our chests and leaped off the concrete edge, puncturing the water's skin, hearing a shatter like glass, then liquid dreaming up all around us, enclosed in a primal, chlorinated bath where it was warm and safe. Lying, smeared with creamy sunblock, letting the rays have a go at us, our skin baking brown and sweet as the cinnamon toast I used to eat as a kid. Florida, an oasis, I jumped in and went down. I did the best I could. I tried to stay away from the TV, the Internet, just my kids and crafting. And it was lovely. But there was also something heavy in my gut, in the stomach that so disgusts Trump, the stomach that has been handed down to me by generations of Irish women; it is in my genes. My nana always had this flab of fat on her belly. It is what we are: our bodies.

I was hoping Barbara would call. I expected her to call, to reach out somehow, to explain, console, communicate goddamn it. Just communicate. She did not call. This meant—what else could it mean but guilt—a tacit acknowledgment that in some way, shape, or form she had said those words to Trump. Betrayal—the hardest thing to deal with for us humans.

I wanted to contact her. Would I get a response? I looked at my computer keypad, my phone keypad, my computer keypad, my phone keypad. I went to the pool, walked three times around, went back to the computer, typed in some words: "Dear Rosie; From Barbara," erase. My friends. Who are they? Some are famous; some not. It wouldn't matter. If any friend, be it Jackie or Madonna, had publicly said the things about me that she had, I would have phoned them. I would not have issued a press release. That's what Barbara did. She issued a press release from her boat, in some sea: ". . . I do not regret for one moment my choice to hire Rosie O'Donnell as the moderator of *The View*." The end. Not enough. In real life, not nearly enough.

Well, of course she didn't regret hiring me. I had helped that show, a lot. What I had done to her private life, now that was a whole other matter. I shook up her society crowd—they were not happy—she doesn't like controversy of any kind. Still, I expect more of my friends, and, if not my friends, women in general. I believe in simple sisterhood. I believe in a basic bond, unspoken yet understood, that exists among all women.

⌒

The world is comprised of clubs, and usually people belong to more than one. Walters—she was a feminist, she shattered the glass ceiling, she paved the way, she made the wake wide enough for me; we were in the club of women together. But she was also in the rich money club, the designer gowns and gilded mirrors and yachts in the Riviera club. And when the shit hit the golden fan, she tossed the women's club aside and cast her allegiance with the wealthy guy. I don't believe in that world. It has no value to me—at all. And this may be one reason why Trump was so enraged. Not only had I threatened his manhood—me, a degenerate, obese lesbian—to him this is unfathomable—but a woman like me had had the gall to criticize him, to claim he'd been bankrupt, to say he'd made his fortune from Papa, that pageants are innately misogynistic, that he is a pompous idiot. How dare I? As for Barbara, she had to choose. And when she did, the grand illusion, the movie in my mind, the possibility of sisterhood, of bonds that cannot be broken—that movie—ended there, Christmas week.

∾

These are hard harsh judgments, I know. And judgments equally hard and harsh could be made of me. My hypocrisy, for instance, my constant criticism of fame and money and my unwillingness to give either up. My superwoman save-the-day narcissism that says it serves everyone but oftentimes serves mostly me. I know my flaws. I'm willing to admit them or hear them. Every flaw is an essential part of the prism. From one direction it's a mistake. Tilt it to the right, though, let the sun shine on it now, and it glows with integrity.

∾

Kelli and I took the kids out for dinner. There was a brand-new restaurant that had opened. Vivi was excited; she skipped down the street ahead of us, chanting "out to dinner." This place had a sports bar feel to it, and there were TVs everywhere, everywhere. I didn't want to see a TV. That was my only requirement of any restaurant.

Spit in the food, burn the burgers; it's all fine so long as you didn't have a goddamn TV. The maitre d' must have seen the look of horror on my face. He said, "I'll take you upstairs." So we went upstairs where there were far fewer customers, and only one TV, which was the size of the Great Wall of China, but going low. A sports channel was on. "Okay," I thought, "we will be safe."

Well, wouldn't you know it, but then there we were; we popped up, Rosie vs. Trump. Our faces were huge, and the screen was split, me on one side, Donald on the other, and we were each blown up so big, with a ticker tape running underneath us, and, well you know what I'm going to say. Where, oh where, was the world? I just can't get my mind around the fact that this is news. Why is this news on a sports channel?! I can only surmise people watch this stuff because it distracts them from knowing the real news, which is just too heavy to handle.

Anyway, Blake looked up at the screen. And he said, "You know what, Mom? Kyle said that you were going to get sued by some guy who has dump trucks and Kyle said the dump truck guy is going to take all your money."

"No no no," I said.

Vivi said, "If he takes all your money, we will beat him up!"

"Vivi," I said, "we are not going to beat anyone up. Beating up is not nice. You don't beat up people and he's not going to take our money. He's just being a bully. You know why, I teased him on TV, and he didn't like it. He's a rich kid and he is spoiled."

"Like Malfoy?" Parker asked.

From *Harry Potter*. Exactly.

Parker said, "I heard he said the 'f' word about you!"

In our house, the "f" word is *fat*.

My children know their mama is fat, and that their mama feels bad about this, although I have tried, for their sake, not to hide who I am. They see. They know. In Florida my legs brown only up to my knees, my arms to my biceps. My face turns the color of toast, though, a nice healthy hue; I like my face okay. It feels somehow not connected to my body.

So that Christmas week, Trump was spewing on every talk show out there about how disgusting I was, such a slob, a pig. The result of which was everyone, whether they knew me or not, telling me I looked lovely. I never got so many compliments in my life than that week I was in Florida. People I didn't know would come up to me and say, "Just so you know, we think you look great!" I'd be walking down the street in Miami and little old ladies would come up to me and touch my cheeks and say, "Honey, you look good," or "Sweetheart, you know you're gorgeous." It touched me, the fundamental urge people have to salve someone who is wounded. It was an urge exactly the opposite of Trump's, which was to attack. "You're beautiful," people kept saying. "Beautiful." Abundant kindness.

But sometimes there is nothing anyone can do or say that will penetrate the leaden ball sitting in the stomach. It was there. I tried as best I could to be with my kids, because this was my time, a stretch of time, a rare occurrence. I tried. But the heaviness, the anger, I often needed to retreat from. My children wanted to know why Mama was in the craft room so much.

I was in there gluing things together. The glue felt good. I liked the tacky feeling on my fingers. I liked to press the pads of my coated fingertips together, wait a moment, and then pry them apart, watch the half-dried Elmer's stretch its clear coating before snapping in half. I glued boxes inside boxes inside boxes, a world collapsing to a cube so small it could barely be measured; that's what I was making. I glued plastic fighting figures, soldiers on a ledge with a flag draped behind them, the red not stripes but scrawl, the stars van Gogh-ish, hypnotic hysterical swirls of silver and white. I could not stop gluing. I used Elmer's and Mod Podge and Krazy Glue. I glued a block to the ceiling, standing on a step stool for the requisite half hour, giving the glue time to dry. It was the embodiment of how I felt. Precarious. Dangerous. About to fall. But not.

It was January now, back East the days gray, the trees stark and nude, but in Florida every day was a soft balmy blue. Why could I not feel it, appreciate it? This

hurt me, the fact that I could not be hurt, that somewhere inside I was numbed out and automatic. And
despite the distance between me and Barbara, she on her
yacht on the other side of some sea, and then back in
Manhattan ready to resume her seat on the show, while
I was here, "vacationing" with my brood, despite the
distance I felt in some weird way like Barbara was with
me, almost literally *on* my mind. I swam in the pool. I
carried on long elaborate conversations with Barbara; I
told her about my childhood; we talked politics; I explained to her how much it hurt, her carefully crafted
truce attempts, her palm not out in the form of gift-
giving, but up, like a policeman, his white glove a blank
mute *stop. Stop!* What would have stopped it for me
was her start, her offer to step to my side, sisterhood,
the mutual need to preserve and protect. For some
reason, as I swam, or walked, or sang my kids to sleep,
I kept recalling a dinner we had well before *The View*
started. So it must have been—what—that summer before September 5, or even earlier, in the spring. Barbara
asked Kelli and me out to dinner, this while the contract
negotiations were probably going on, and we went. Of
course we went. Kelli looked as Kelli always does look,
simply, cleanly, casually elegant. Here's the thing. Usually I care not a whit about clothes. I dress the way I
need to, and when I don't need to, I dress in whatever's
comfortable. But that night, getting ready to dine with
Barbara, I thought about what to wear. I stood in front

of my closet and fingered the pants, the cotton shirts. I wanted to look right for Barbara, and what would that mean? A sequined gown, a high-end suit? No. Not me. At all. In the end I chose khakis and J. Jill clogs. I chose clothes that at once reflected who I was but that would also appeal to her aesthetic: tailored; tasteful. From the very beginning, I think, I have wanted to both be who I am and who she wanted me to be.

Why am I so young, even as I age?

What was I doing on January 3, 2007, at 11 a.m. eastern standard time? I don't know. I was definitely not watching the television; that much I know, because the last thing I wanted during my vacation was more media. Maybe I was taking a walk with Vivi. Maybe I was in our boat, in the Floridian bay, looking for seahorses with Blake. Blake is the most magical of my children; everywhere he goes he finds unlikely objects: a copper key, a tiny crystal car, a perfectly preserved sand dollar. Lately he had been interested in seahorses, searching for them everywhere, and I went with him. I looked up seahorses on Google; maybe I was doing that on January 3, 2007, at 11 a.m. eastern standard time, typing the word *seahorse* into the search box and seeing scroll down my screen the mythical miniature beast with its curved blade of a body. Seahorses, I read, that day or sometime soon thereafter, seahorses are some of the animal kingdom's most venerable males. After the females lay their eggs, the fathers take them into their mouths, gestating them there for the time it takes, holding their young in their soft sealed maws until they hatch. I wasn't sure of that fact; didn't the males hold the eggs in pouches? Hadn't I learned that somewhere? It didn't matter right then, what mattered to me was the image of females roaming free in the ocean while the males toil for the newborns, gently spitting them into the sea once they hatch, so they are cradled in the waves. I like seahorses. They make Homo-sapien males, like Trump, at the least less inevitable. If men were like seahorses, maybe Barbara and I, maybe all women, would not have such tangled, tough relationships.

So, let's say I was reading about seahorses that day, that time, January 3, Barbara now back from vacation and taking her seat at the table again. I did not see the show and I'm glad for that, because I'm not sure what I would have done had I witnessed her essentially communicating with me through the camera, in public, choosing to explain to me her thoughts, her position, her sentiments, with such a broad brush. What I wanted was what any sane person would have wanted: an intimate heart-to-heart, but Barbara doesn't do intimacy. I do, or at least I try, although it's true I fail over three quarters of the time. But one thing's for sure: even with all my interpersonal faults, I would not use the television to attempt conflict resolution with a friend or a colleague.

Which is what she did. Instead of speaking with me

on the phone, or writing me a long letter, she went on air, January 3rd, 11 a.m., and, from what I later heard, said blah dedidi dah dedididah. Supposedly she read a carefully crafted statement all strategy, no heart. "... *clearing things up ... Donald Trump ... not happy with my decision ... the truth ... never regretted ... hiring ... clearing things up ... truth ... clearing things up ...*"

Nothing. It clarified nothing for me. If anything it made it worse. Because, like I said, my way of doing dialogue, of negotiating relationships, of working through fights, is not to address the person in question on the tube. But that's how Barbara does it. That's how she's done it her whole life. Think of that. Practically her whole life on air. Way up high, in the thinness. What a wingspan! But how hard it is to breathe.

"Write to her," Kelli said once we'd heard what she'd said. "Don't tell her you didn't watch it," Kelli said. "Just write to her and say, 'Thank you for the show today. Let's put this behind us and start the New Year. Rosie.'"

I tried. I typed it out. I kept staring at the screen. *New Year. Rosie. Thank you for the show.*

Thank you for the show.

Five simple words, every one a single syllable. Those words kept clacking in my head. Thank you for the show. I couldn't say it. Couldn't send it. Stuck.

I was due back on *The View* January 8. So I had five

more days left with my family. I tried to put all problems out of my head. We went out on our boat; we barbecued. We played Scrabble. We loved each other. The kids played with their Christmas presents and fought endlessly about Blake's electric car, a miniature automobile that he could race around the driveway in, vroom, around he went, in circles, over and over again, hour after hour. What he was doing on the outside was what was happening in my head on the inside, around and around, electricity crackling, the synapses sparking, even though it was over. I knew it was not. For betrayal is deep. It is the fish flailing and it can't get air. It's epic, movie-esque. It is primitive and painful in a way that defies words. Time does not always heal. With time it got worse, not Donald, but Barbara, and the hurt, and the rage, five-fingered, fisted, too hot to touch.

Blake circled madly in his brand-new car; he would not stop. "Enough!" I screamed at him one afternoon. He stopped abruptly, pressed the pedal, and came screeching to a halt. He looked up at me, confused. "What?" he said. How could I explain that I wasn't yelling at him? I was yelling at me. "Sorry, dude," I said, touching his head. "Brain fart," I said. He threw back his head and laughed. And I saw a look on his face I have captured a thousand times in his seven years on earth. It stills my soul. Smiling. He sped away.

She betrayed me in many ways, my mother. First off, she died. Disappeared like a Copperfield trick. For years I lived in a dream, waiting to wake. She just up and left, and didn't give me directions as to how to find her. I looked for years. I am still looking. Lauren Slater shares the same birthday with me. I have many similarities with Slater, so when we discovered we shared the same birthday, it was weird. "What time were you born?" she asked. As if I would know. I do not know. I never have. I doubt I ever will.

She was vibrant, my mother was. She was size ten, I think, rough around the edges, pretty pleasant/ peasant-looking. She had a loud voice and a huge humor to hide her too huge heart. She could make you laugh, Roseann O'Donnell, and she did make you laugh. Schoolteachers at Rolling Hills Elementary School, Commack, Long Island, will tell you this. I still know them now. Miss Boy, Miss Leiner—young, smart, feminist women, they were maybe twenty-one, my mother thirty-five or thirty-six. She would have them doubled over laughing in the hallway. My mom was a star; really, she was.

My mother knew beauty; she knew talent. She loved Broadway and passed that love on to me. She loved show business, and seeing the stars on a stage. She was strong, my mom, very powerful, at least to me, in my mind.

I was ten when she died. And maybe because I was a child, she will be a certain way in my mind.

But now, as an adult, as a mom myself, I wonder why she made the choices she did. I want to know her, find her friends, find anyone who remembers a moment alone with her when something real happened between them. I want some random snapshot, some photos of my mother, and I have very few. I have only two, I think.

After she died I snuck into my parents' room to look through her box of photos, memories she kept of her life. There was talk of who would get them. There were so few things. Her stuff went missing, like she did.

In the summer of 1973, after my mother died, my dad took us to Northern Ireland to visit his family, whom he didn't really know at all, he a widower with five kids, taking them all to Ireland on his own.

Northern Ireland, greener than green, but the color didn't come to me. Because after she left, it got all gray and dark. The memory of her color did not return to me for years and years, did not return until I held my son Parker for the first time.

I held him and . . . Oh yes. I remember this. Something stuttering to a start, deep in my brain, an ancient recollection, a feeling without words—I held my son. And I recalled what it meant, or felt, to be adored. And that is how I know she adored me. I know my mother's love because it is her love that pours through me and allows me to adore the look on Blake's face when I say *brain fart* or how it feels to take a tub with a two-year-old. What a relief it was, for me to have my children, to know I knew how to love a baby, because I was a baby loved.

I can find forgiveness because I am a mother now—with two daughters of my own. What were my mother's choices, really? No work, no way of making money; it was a different era then. I forgive my mother. I forgive her for not protecting me in all the ways I wish she would have. I forgive her for chopping down the tree when I told her that at night a man was climbing that tree and coming in my window. I forgive her for her failure of interpretation, her literal response to my metaphorical truth. The tree came down. With it went its leaves, its roots, the circular lifelines in its flesh. When she left, a part of me went with her.

✑

We returned to Nyack on January 7. The next day, I went in to work. And I was thinking, "How am I going to do this?" If there was one time in my life when I could have used an IFB, this would have been it. I wanted an IFB and I wanted Kelli to be in the control room, talking in my ear, telling me what to say when I spoke to Barbara. I was feeling ragged and raw. Her words. "Donald is a good friend of the show . . ." Those words convey no truths.

✑

Every day, when I arrived at ABC, I rode the elevator down and went into my dressing room. There in front of me were three words in huge letters—*All My Children*—and every day these words made me smile.

All My Children. Every day at *The View* I saw those words as I settled into my dressing room. And then, once I was settled, I would meet with the other co-hosts and some staff in the hair and makeup room, which I always thought was the oddest place to have a formal discussion, but there it was.

That day was no different. I went to my dressing room. I read the three words. Then I walked down the long white barren corridor on the third floor of ABC, a surprisingly shabby corridor in a surprisingly shabby building whose slick exterior belies none of what it truly contains. The white walls are scuffed here and there, and the ceilings are made of those foam industrial tiles. There are no windows in these hallways. They wind through the building like old intestines, doorways opening on either side to reveal dressing rooms with framed portraits of soap opera celebrities, or empty rooms with ugly love seats, the backs shaped like hearts, the pillows gray.

I walked into the hair and makeup room and took my usual seat. There were, as always, hair dryers in their holsters bolted to the chrome counters and plastic bins full of spiky rollers and tarnished clips. There were combs of every shape and size, combs clutching the hairs of the rich and famous, brittle hairs leeched of color from years of chemical treatments.

I picked up a comb. I have no idea why. I sat in my usual seat, staring straight ahead, a large pebble in my gut, and I clutched a comb clutching hairs, which are the saddest things sometimes, hairs loosened from a human head. Stray hairs, damaged hairs, the tiny, almost microscopic-but-not-quite bulbs at their tips where they were once joined with the follicles from which they sprouted. Did you know that humans have used almost every type of animal hair there is to make brushes for painting? From the beginning humans have been so eager to paint—cave paintings make this obvious—that they have probably taken hair from you name it—foxes, squirrels, maybe even skunks—and bound them together, stuck them to sticks, and dipped them in the ground pigment of fruits and flowers. Why, I have always wondered, why has no one ever tried to make a brush using human hair? What would a picture painted with a human hair brush look like? Would it feel more real? Would the picture leap to life, and start to smell of apple, or daisies? Hair. I clutched the comb clutching the hairs and I saw how easily we are split.

My heart was pounding. My heart was clattering like the shitty cart at Target, the wheel wobbling around, and I thought, "Here is the beginning of a panic attack."

From the corner of my eye, I could see that Barbara was already in the room.

∼

And it was 1971, and I was at the breakfast table, and there was my mother in her fuzzy slippers and her electric blue almost velour zip-up nightgown. It was morning, and we were acting as if everything was all right, but it wasn't. What was wrong? I don't know. Even today I can't say, because I'm not sure, because my memories are more in feeling than form. Maybe nothing happened, except in my mind. It almost doesn't matter, because our minds are all we have; our whole worlds. I remember searching for a way to say a thing I could neither see nor understand. "A man came in my room at night and got me," I told my mother.

I remember her asking me how he got into my room, and I remember telling her he got in through the window above my bed, which had a tree next to it. I told her he climbed the tree, climbed and climbed.

I must have been very convincing, because she had the neighbor, Mike, cut down that tree. Mike had us all hold hands and watch the tree tip, tip, and fall. Its crown came crashing down.

"There," she said. "Now he can't get in."

But he did. And when I told her that, she said,

"Roseann, you lie like a rug." And I thought, "Mom, rugs can't talk."

Can they?

I learned not to talk. I learned not to bring the sore subject up, because her face, well, the look on her face when I told her he was still getting in, and when she told me I lied like a rug, that look on her face was something I never wanted to see again.

My childhood was spent doing whatever I could to avoid that look, to avoid the words that could cause such an expression of—of what?—to cross the features of my mother's face. I lay, indeed, like a rug. I flattened out. I kept quiet. I ate my cereal at the breakfast table every morning, sitting there surrounded by words and Froot Loops, so much unsaid.

～

And then Barbara got up from sitting, because she was getting her hair washed, and walked over with a towel on her head and she put her arms around me from behind. She didn't look at me. She looked at my reflection in the mirror and my reflection in the mirror looked at her reflection in the mirror, so we were and were not facing each other. Our reflections were facing each other; no, I would not do mirror to mirror.

I stood up. I tell people I love, have always told

them: if ever you are in a fight with me and I stand up, leave the room. Not because I'm going to hit you—I have never hit a person and I have never worried that I would. But if I stand up that's a sign that the rage is too big for my body. I have to move, to readjust the rage and the pressure of the past, so I did. I just got out of my makeup chair, my eyes full of teary rage, and she was standing, not in a chair, and her hair was wet.

If human beings were dogs, Barbara would for sure be an alpha. I stood up, and was therefore violating her authority. I could feel how in a single instance her whole soul became an exclamation point, a mandate: *Sit! Stay! Roll over! Come!* In my mind I could hear her voice, the voice I'd been hearing since I was a little girl, way back on Rhonda Lane, watching this woman on the TV. She was so much younger then, and gorgeous through and through; she still is. Her voice is resonant, a bell so full of itself its echoes are visible, dense quivering rings of re-peats, words that will be heard. Barbara's voice, her entire being, has never failed to instill in the listener a sense of awe, of fear. Only now, I sensed she could sense her effect was wavering, because I wasn't feeling awe, I wasn't feel-ing fear; it all took just a single split second, confusion, and then uncertainty flashing across her face.

"Why did you not call me?" I said. "For ten days you didn't call."

I looked at her. She was, and probably always will be, so hard to read, but I thought I could see it, or sense it really, a struggle inside, the need to maintain composure.

"Ten goddamn days," I said, my voice now low and cruel. I paused. "You're a liar."

"Stop," I heard a voice somewhere inside me say, but the voice was so low, I did not stop. I do what I always do when wounded. I go for the tender spot. "A liar." I said this to a journalist whose job it is to tell the truth.

"I did everything I could," said Barbara, "everything I could to squash the story."

I didn't believe her. How could I? The fact is, she is less than truthful in so many ways—everything she could? And for a second, right there in that makeup room, January, 2007, I had the feeling of hating her, but in hating her, I could see, I was also hating myself.

"Everything I could," she said—and in my mind I was thinking, *everything? Nothing. You did what you needed to do to protect your hide.*

We yelled, the staff stared, I tried very hard not to cry. We each took some shots, some hurtful, some primitive.

I must admit, she was a fantasy mother for me. This fantasy, I have it over and over again, with women I respect who are old enough to be my mother, to truly be her, the missing one.

Why do we never stop wanting to be loved like a child? Why do we never stop wanting to be so small?

"You're a liar," I said again, wishing I wouldn't. My anger embarrasses me.

Barbara was looking at me, her face at once devastated and curious.

"Stop," Bill Geddie said, or did I just imagine this? I was shaking, in a blur. So, I believe, was Barbara.

And then it was over. Somehow it ended. Time's up. We were due on air. Right now. So we went out to that table, the set. During the fight, all nine of us had been in the room. The show watching the show. And then it was time to go. Oh well. Who said you can't do a TV show where no one likes each other? *The View* hosts had been doing that for the past nine years.

We all got up, out of our seats. We rode the elevator up to the set, the one I had helped design—it felt like so long ago, last July, a lifetime ago, I had such hope then. And such hope after Streisand too. That hope was gone now. My view of *The View* had dilated, then contracted, and was squeezing smaller still.

We went onto the set. Imagine us. Four whitewashed women, our eyes startled, Barbara I believe probably wrecked behind her mask of makeup. We sat in our assigned seats. The tiny microphones were, as always, pinned to our lapels, the IFBs lodged in everyone's ears except mine. I could hear. I have always been able to hear exceptionally well. Sometimes I think I have some kind of autistic streak. I can hear the sound of laughter from far away. I can hear creeping in the night. I can hear the sound of water washing down the drain from two rooms over, the sound of Kelli turning a page of the novel she is reading five hundred feet from me. But I could not hear Zoë caught in the car. I could not hear her fear or her despair, even when it was right up against me. Some sounds are so intense, some griefs so deep, they register in a key too pure and full for the compromised human ear. My ears. They were ringing. My head. Dizzy.

Welcome to *The View*!

"Wow, how was that," Joy said, starting off the show, an absurd but appropriate beginning to an absurd but appropriate show, a show that showed us bombed out by strife, trying to cover.

I snuck a look at Barbara. My heart hurt. I hate to pretend.

"I dunno," I said, forcing myself into my mode, the role. Those were my first words uttered on *The View* when I returned.

"Well, I don't know, I gotta tell you something, it was pretty intense, I think I hit a nerve with that guy!"

I never said his name.

"Let me say definitively," Barbara said, "that everything he said I said about her is totally untrue." To me, it looked like she was visibly struggling. She looked into the camera. She read the prompter. These were the words. True or false, your call. Later, Barbara said, "that poor pathetic man," which is a very vague statement, a statement about Donald, about herself, or about people, plain people, here and there, or everywhere.

CHAPTER 12

You Know Where I Am

Two memories:
1

After I left my first show, I was shocked at the freedom. I now had the time to e-mail friends, and to take long baths too. In our house we have an under-four rule. If you're under four you can bathe with Mama. Chelsea had turned five recently. Viv still an infant, that left me and my baby Blake. Tonight, we were having bubbles, Willie, a killer whale, lined up on the ledge with the great white and the blue. It was 2003. At that time, Blake was three, and all whales were killer whales.

Our tub was not normal. It was shaped like a figure eight with two levels; an adult and a three-year-old could fit without a problem. Blake was on the seat, the ledge they designed for rich women to shave their legs, and I was on the bottom. My tummy was hovering just above the water's rim, like two hippos barely submerged.

He kicked at it, the hippos, my belly. I just watched. Then another kick. Then a pause.

"Mama, why you tummy so big?" Blake asked. I smiled, and said, "Because I eat too much food." And Blake said, "Me no like it," and I said, "Me no like it either." And that was that. Willie did a triple jump and we both got out and dried off and got into our new matching pajamas. Thank God for Target.

The next day at breakfast, I told the story to Kel, and Geraldine, and anyone who would listen, and everyone laughed. Blake looked a little ashamed.

The next night, Blake and I bathed again. The water was perfect, the superheroes lined up. He stared at my stomach, again, and after a moment of direct eye contact he said, "Mama, I like your big tummy."

"Do you feel bad 'cause everyone laughed when I told the story?" I asked, and he nodded. At three, he felt it, the subtle, self-deprecating shame wrapped in humor. And he was telling me that he can love even the parts of me others hate; that he can love even the parts of me he himself hates. We hugged.

Your children heal you.

2

I got the idea by accident, the first time I fell off my bike. The bike was new, a birthday present. My dad took me to pick it out. I wanted a bike like Jackie's: small, pink, with streamers coming out of the handlebars. They didn't have any like Jackie's. I kept looking. My dad started sweating. I had to pick one quickly, before he changed his mind or got fed up, before my already ruined eleventh birthday became a total washout. I chose a burnt-orange banana bike, without streamers. It was too big and not at all what I was looking for. By eleven, I was used to that.

When Jackie got her new bike, her dad let her ride it home from the fire station. He drove behind her with flashers on, all the way up Marie Crescent. I asked if I could ride my bike home, like Jackie had. My dad said no. My mother was dead by then. She would have let me ride home, at least from the sump. I was sure.

There was sand in the street, left over from the melted snow. Spring had just arrived. My mom had been buried. I was cruising the neighborhood on my nowhere near perfect bike. I tried to skid, like the cool kids did, and fell off. I landed on my wrist. It hurt, a lot.

I ran, holding my wounded hand in my healthy one. I left my bike in the middle of the street and I ran. Where to run? That was the question. Not many choices: no Mom, Dad at work, a nana who couldn't see, hear, or drive a car. I ran to a neighbor, Mrs. Nordin. She took me to get an X-ray, then on to Dr. Reichmann's office, where I got my first cast. I got all kinds of attention. No gifts, though. I expected gifts.

When Howie Nordin got a cast, he got gifts. Howie got his foot caught in the escalator at E.J. Korvette's. He was seven, wearing new sneakers; the laces got caught first, and then the whole sneaker got pulled under the metal moving steps. Howie started to scream, and so did his mom. Then, a miracle. Some man standing behind the Nordins jumped on the escalator handrail, slid down to the very bottom, and hit the "emergency stop" button. The ambulance arrived, the paramedics with crowbars, and they set his foot free. Howie went to the hospital and got a big cast on his leg. Everyone said he would have been killed were it not for the man who knew all about the emergency stop button. The man saved him, then disappeared just like Superman.

All the neighborhood kids watched as Howie was carried from the car, cast and all. We went to see him the next day, to give him his get well presents. We walked in without knocking, as usual. I couldn't believe my eyes; it looked like Christmas, presents everywhere!

We bought him the Gunfight at O.K. Corral shooting gallery. I picked it out myself, because it was the best toy I had ever seen in my whole entire life, next to Rock 'Em Sock 'Em Robots. The Corral was $24 but my father bought it anyway because he always got sweaty and nervous in stores and I knew how to use that to my advantage. Howie got gifts. I got nothing.

I had a broken arm, and no mother, and still no toys. I went to school the next day, white cast in a sling, Magic Markers ready. I was reborn. I went from the horrific "kid with a dead mom" to the interesting "kid with a cast." It was like a miracle. Eyes formerly filled with pity and sadness now brimmed with curiosity and intrigue.

"Can I sign it? How do you take a bath? Will they saw it off?" These statements had replaced, "Think she's a ghost following you around? Think maggots are eating her eyeballs right now? Think your dad's gonna die and you'll be an orphan?" It was intoxicating and it was addictive. I had proof of my pain, white and heavy, for all to see. Proof I was being cared for and tended to, that I was worth taking care of. Proof that I had some value, enough to be fixed. And I found I wasn't sad anymore. I was distracted. I had a new pain to focus on, one that was easier to heal than the original. There were many benefits to having a cast. In the middle of the night, it was a weapon.

I broke many bones after that first one, mostly by myself, in my bedroom, with a heavy wooden hanger or a small Mets baseball bat I got at bat day. My hands and fingers usually. No one knew. My secret.

My shrink tells me that that was how I survived, how I learned to cope, as a child. It no longer serves me. Even now, just remembering it, just writing it down, makes it more real than I want it to be. Acquired long before I had a voice, I cannot shake it, this longing for someone to salve what cannot be seen.

I never dream of her.

I would like to see her, one last time. Some night, Mom.

You know where I am.

CHAPTER 13

Two Faces

After Barbara disavowed him on *The View*, Donald went screeching back to the media. "She lied . . . and now she has chosen to lie again." I don't think I watched it. I heard about it. I was spending the night with my kids. Sometimes, instead of telling them stories before bed, I'll come up and sing them each a special song. Vivi loves this the best. Someone once asked me: which child is most like you? And I answered, Vivi.

I saw Viv get born. I had not been there from the beginning with any of my others, and this is something special. I certainly don't love her more than any of my others. I love them all fiercely and differently, and one of these differences is that I have known Viv since . . . since when? I inseminated Kelli. I was there at Vivi's conception, side by side with Kel, or cooking dinner; at what moment did the sperm knock at the door of the choosy egg, and at what moment did the egg decide to invite him in for tea? I think I know. But I won't tell.

I saw Viv every step of the way. I saw her heartbeat first, a tiny light, a star from another galaxy, lonely looking. I saw her spine when she was still an embryo, interlocking bones ridging a floating wraith. I noted day 36, when the last of the teeth came in, day 42, when all five fingers were formed; day 240, when she made her blood-speckled entrance, carved from Kelli's stomach under a huge surgical sun. I was the first to hold her, to smell her, to sing her a little song. That song entered her, a transfusion of me to her, and she took it into her marrow. Vivi is a performer, a joker, a character, a comedienne. I sing to her, she to me. Already she loves to belt out Broadway tunes. That night, after *The View*, I was getting ready to put my kids to bed, and Viv was dancing for me on the living room couches, leaping from couch to couch, turning in the air, taking a sweeping proud bow while I clapped and clapped, for Viv. Vivienne. Means life. *L'chaim*. To life.

I was oddly happy, despite the wreckage of the day. Because, as horrible as the fight between Barbara and me had been, it also pulled us together, forced the flesh in a relationship that had been comprised mostly of air. I saw her. She saw me. We got past the reflections, into the core of the common ache. And the world is that much less lonely when the ache is shared.

I put my kids to bed. I read. Sunrise. Sunset. Next

thing I knew, the following afternoon, or two, I got a call from my brother Eddie, who is helping to run my business. My publicist, Cindi Berger, was with him, and they were in the car, racing to my house, an emergency, hold tight, prepare yourself, something bad had happened. They couldn't finish their explanation. The line went dead, dropped the way cell phones sometimes do, which is why I hate them. Hate them! Because there I was, standing in the middle of my kitchen on a late afternoon in the darkest, dirtiest part of the year when the last of the snow is stained, and the grime sticks to your skin. Something terrible had happened. I paced back and forth. I picked up the phone, punched the keypad, bleep bleep bleep. Fuck. Punched again. Bleep bleep bleep. No one else was home with me, no one to say, "Slow down, it's okay," and so my mind ran away. "One of my kids," I thought, and could not finish the sentence. *One of my kids.*

I am funny, very funny, right? But that humor comes from fear. Not fear of Trump, not fear of failure. My fear is of loss. It's the stuck-in-your-gut nameless fear that comes from the curse of the frontal lobes: our knowledge of death. When you are a mother, the death you so much fear is no longer your own.

Every year, Kelli and I take a dreaded vacation.

Here's the problem. I hate vacations. To vacate. To go empty. That's what that means.

Last time we went to Mexico. I was trying to finish a book when one of the staff members approached us on the beach. "Phone," he said. I looked over at Kel. It had happened, no doubt. A crisis of epic proportion. My children. A child. What?

Kel got up and walked into the hotel lobby, avoiding my eyes. I interpreted this to mean she had to look away from me, because she was scared too. I absolutely knew it. Our life as we have lived it was ending.

It took her about eleven minutes to come back to the reading spot. I knew this because I did Mississippi to sixty eleven times. I do not wear a watch.

Now Kel was walking toward me very slowly. She didn't want to alarm me; it was obvious. She was trying to put the sentences together in a way I would be able to hear. I would scream, pound my chest, and try to drown myself in the sea as soon as she gave me the news. No eye contact yet, this was worse than I expected. She stared at the ground and came around her chair, wiping the sand off the towel. "Stalling," I thought. "She must be stalling." She wouldn't even look at me!

Now, my heart was about to explode. I deserved this, whatever it was. The moment stretched to an eternity. Kel sat down, closed her eyes.

"What?" I screamed at her.

"What what?" she said calmly.

"The phone," I grunted through gritted teeth.

"The plane is at ten," she said, "instead of nine."

Then she picked up her Oprah Book Club novel and resumed reading.

I watched her. She sat totally unaware of all I had just been through. She read, my Kelli, my happy, non-neurotic partner. Thank God for her. She does not think that by some miracle of fate we were once again spared, but only for a moment. She thinks we are basically safe. I think so long as we have children we will always be living on the ledge.

⁓

At last they arrived, Eddie and Cindi, breathless, red-faced, and rushed. "What what?" I screamed at them as they burst in through my front door. Cindi whipped a newspaper out of her briefcase, shook it open, spread it on the counter, then stepped back solemnly for me to see. What could it be?

I stepped forward, bent over the counter to read. It was an open letter to me, written by Trump and republished in the paper. All the usual stuff . . . maniacal . . . foolish . . . self-destructive. It pretty much nailed Barbara in terms of times and places, what she supposedly said here and there, what she supposedly said dining at Le Cirque. I looked away from the paper, toward Cindi and my brother. "Don't ever, ever do this to me again," I said.

"It's Donald fucking Trump! Who gives a shit? Cindi, don't tell me you have to come all the way to my house with my brother, unless it is something real! Don't do it! Because I panicked!"

I went into my study. The others followed me, Cindi and Eddie and now Kelli too, who had come home. I blocked them out of my mind. Mentally, I was alone in my study.

Cindi kept saying things like "Barbara's so upset. Barbara is waiting, she's worried, she doesn't know how we will continue on with the show, after what happened today, now this, now that, chitchat . . ." I wasn't listening. I sat down at my desk. I opened my e-mail.

"Dear Barbara Walters," I wrote. "I forgive you and I hope you forgive me. I LOVE U. Rosie"

I sent it and in what seemed like just a few seconds later, her response arrived back. "I'm crying and thank you and I love you."

I went in the next day. I saw her. I was in my dressing room and she knocked. She closed the door after her, a soft click. "Rosie," she said, "before I read that letter in the paper, I never knew how it felt for you."

"Oh God, the letter," I said. "I don't care about Donald Trump, Barbara. I don't care what he says. I don't care anything about him. What I care is this: that you did not defend me. And I have been a good, loyal daughter to you. And I want you to be a good mother to me. Don't let the bad man hurt me." I felt something sore in my throat. I tried to swallow. "It reminds me too much of my childhood," I said.

"Let me bring in Bill Geddie," Barbara said. I smiled inside myself then. I understood Barbara well now. When I first began this job, I might have interpreted her desire to bring her producer into a private talk as a sign of her crassness, her deafness in the interpersonal realm. And to some degree that interpretation might be right. But there's more. Love, loss, fear, vulnerability, connection, these are too hard for her to hold. She is not indifferent to these things, just unskilled and, oddly enough, too raw. Barbara Walters, arguably the most poised person on this planet, all rough-edged and unfinished inside.

"No," I said. I tried to say it gently. "Please. Listen, this is not about anything but you and me. And I'm sorry if I scared you yesterday. I'm sorry that I yelled at you like that . . . And I didn't mean to," I said.

And then we stopped saying anything at all. We stood there, two quiet women, in a dressing room, behind us racks and racks of garments, on the counter a flung-open makeup case, ovals of rouge, big mop brushes beige with powder designed to hide the real foundation of the face. We stood, two women, separated by time and class and circumstance, but linked by things we could neither classify nor price but that were as real as sound, or light, or song.

CHAPTER 14

The Fame Game

Anna Nicole Smith died. I commented about her on air and three hours later my publicist called and told me she was dead. "Oh dear God," I said. Her death affected me in many ways. Anna Nicole Smith was the embodiment of celebrity-hood at its worst. Say that word—*celebrity*. That word should be banished from the dictionary. It is misleading, gives the impression that there is such a thing as a single, stand-alone person who is a celebrity. But a celebrity is not a person; it is a phenomenon, a mixture of one human being and the culture that views her. A celebrity cannot exist without her audience.

This is why I hold the audience responsible in part for Anna Nicole Smith's death. Fame is what killed that girl, and not only did America watch her demise, America abetted it, by either saying nothing or, worse, tuning in. There is something deeply wrong with a country that feeds off the drunken descent of a person who, two days after a C-section, wound still open and bloody, swims in the sea while the cameramen watch. Why did no one say, "Stop!" Why did no one say, "Good God, you could go septic?" Part of the fear is that what happened to her could happen to me.

Celebrity-hood is not a real place. There are no parties there. Celebrity-hood is an intersection that occurs in the air somewhere between the viewer and the viewed. And everyone knows that intersections are where most automobile accidents happen; they are dangerous dicey places of near misses, sudden swerves, and sirens. If you approach the intersection with nothing on your side except speed, as Anna Nicole did, you are a likely candidate for a crash. I try to remember this. To live well in this intersection, you must have some real skill, an ability to carry you through.

I am a comedienne. My talent is linked to laughter. My core desire is to connect with people in the raw realness of their lives. I always remember this, that my work is about connection, and timing; about story, revelation, and comfort. So long as I remember what I am basically about, I cannot be hurt in the intersection. Once I forget this, though, and lean on sheer speed as my asset, I know I will go down, while you, my friend, just watch.

The View was a roller-coaster ride the likes of which I had never experienced before. For one year I moved into a house that was already occupied by its owners, that had the stamp of their style everywhere. Their style was not, and still is not, mine. I like plain soft cotton, just washed denim, big faded flowers on schlumpy couches. I like textiles with some history, beautiful mosaics, furniture that has the wear from a hundred hands.

I tried to change the style—after all, it was my house now too—but I didn't want to be insulting, even as I could not bear the plastic wrap covering their couches. And while some people maintain that all taste, all styles, are equally valid, I am not such a relentless relativist. The fact is, plastic wrap covering your couch is ugly, and if millions of others are going to have to see it, it becomes uglier still. My year at *The View* was about, in part, trying to build a better house without insulting the current carpenters, who have real skills but bad tools.

The IFB is a case in point. Joy and Elisabeth didn't give it up when Barbara went away for Christmas vacation, and, while I was disappointed, I was learning to accept that people change only when they are ready. I was learning that part of art is working with what you have, not chucking it out for better, brighter material. What would Streisand have done? Having found herself in a situation such as mine, unable to leave or to totally take charge, she would have worked with what was in front of her, tuned and tuned, tweaked and tipped, until her touch transformed.

A few weeks after the Barbara blowout, Trump having retreated into his crate and quiet now, sleeping with a blanket thrown over the wire box and kibble by his snoring side, a few weeks later, close to Valentine's Day now, we were going to do a craft segment, "six quick gifts you can make in six minutes," kind of thing. I was going to show how to make these gifts and had it all planned out, my Mod Podge, my red folk-art paint, step one, step two, here's how. The segment before mine was with John Stamos and Anita Baker. Everything was going fine, and we were all relaxed. The fighting between me and Barbara had made things worse in the short term but better overall, like a boil that's burst, it hurt like hell and then emptied.

So we were all relaxed, me and Joy and Elisabeth and Barbara, joking around with John Stamos. Elisabeth was doing what they call the *close*, which is the good-bye. She had her IFB in. And then, instead of finishing up the good-bye according to the teleprompter words, Elisabeth suddenly, and for the first time, swerved. She said to John, "Hey, why don't you stick around and make some crafts with Rosie?" I rolled my eyes, and John said, "What?"

"It'll be fun," Elisabeth said. "Stick around. We'll all have fun."

"Okay," John said, at first a little unsure but then, "Okay, I'll stay!"

I didn't want him to stay, because we had only six minutes to show the audience how to do six crafts. It was all planned out, and an added guest would not help move things along.

I was mad because I'd thought someone up there in the booth had whispered directives into her IFB, directives that had, indeed, screwed up my segment, which was awkward and ill executed because I suddenly had to accommodate a person who scrambled the clear steps I'd planned to describe. But that was not a big deal, not at all, especially if Elisabeth had acted on her own behest. In fact, the big deal was that she had acted on her own behest, scripted Elisabeth suddenly breaking free from the IFB! So what if my craft segment got screwed up? That was a small price to pay if it allowed Elisabeth to break rank.

I didn't have a chance to talk to her after the show. I was rushing home to get my kids from school. I don't know what triggered the feeling. I drove under a bridge where there were pigeons packed in the rafters. Pigeons spook me, and I find it odd that in another context they're doves. I love doves but I dislike pigeons. How could they be the same bird? How can one animal have two names, two types, two meanings? Then again, how can one person have two faces? Now that's a good question. And I was asking this question, dreaming of doves, driving to get my kids.

And all of a sudden, a shadow came over me. It was as though I'd been in warm water and the current went cold. Bam. A bad feeling, a flipped switch. I hate that. Moods and premonitions. I had the sense that Elisabeth was worried. It was as though I could feel her fear, but it was all imagined. Then again, when she had said to Stamos, "stick around and we'll do crafts," I think I saw, in retrospect, a sort of surprise in her eyes, as though she were startled by her own spontaneity. And anyone who has ever struggled in the least bit with any unbidden act, or sudden sadness, or mood-out-of-nowhere knows, it can be frightening, your own mind. Your own capacities. Who knows what will come out of you, unbidden? Who knows how endless your griefs might be? Who knows if the force of your own love might eliminate you? Who knows what words are inside?

Later on, that night, when the house was quiet, I opened up my computer. "Elisabeth," I wrote. "What you did was really okay, a fine thing." I paused, my hands hovering over the keys. I knew Elisabeth used to play softball, and I knew in softball one of the best strategies is to try and steal home. "Remember this." I wrote. "I want you to always steal home. Most people r not brave enough. U r . I want you to take the reins. We r a team, all of us. I trust ur instinct—listen to urself—and when u know u can, steal home."

I was writing her the truth, from my heart. I felt I saw her slowly becoming more real. Well no, not slowly, suddenly. She spoke over her IFB. Plus she had said, on the same show, that she was a binger. You can't get much more real than that. It hurt to hear.

Which is why I wrote, right after that, "Elisabeth. I love you. I will protect you." I knew as soon as I wrote it, it would throw her over the edge. "Elisabeth, I love you and I will protect you."

I sat there for a second and stared at the words. I imagined her receiving them. She would feel happy, she would feel loved, and she would also feel lost. Those words, I knew, would be too much for her, too raw and sudden. She wouldn't know what to do with my feeling of love, which I find odd, because she is a Christian and all Jesus taught was love, but there it is. Should I send this message? And then I did.

And sure enough, for a few days Elisabeth was shy around me, and then the shyness passed and we continued to have our regular run-ins. She continued to appall me with her almost glib comments about torture, and who is right and who is wrong, but the feeling of baseline love stayed. I have always seen inside Elisabeth the artist, the girl who can paint gorgeous pictures, and the athlete, strong arms, strong legs, swift runner, captain. I swear, I heard a slight shift to her voice, a resonance that wasn't there before. I told her I loved her and not long after that she took out her IFB, and hasn't worn it since. She's speaking on her own now. She has her singular voice. I consider this one of my year's major achievements.

Joy followed. Elisabeth took out her IFB and then so did Joy. And there was a softness to Barbara that had not been there before. Or maybe the softness was between us, at the intersection where we crashed, and were wounded, and then slowly, bandaged and infinitely more cautious, approached again.

Because that is what happened. The conflict came to a boiling point and stripped us of our pretense. In my blowup with Barbara I learned that I too have pretense. I had never shown her before my rage, or my fear, and I had never admitted to her what she meant to me, as a maybe-mother. We collided in air, on air, and the force of it tore the armor from us. What I felt, I will never forget. I know now that Barbara's wounded-ness is very deep. Looking at Barbara after our makeup room fight, I was reminded of seeing inside Kelli the day Viv was born. The cream-colored skin was carved open to reveal the wet organs all veined and incredible. Your jaw drops at what lies inside. It is far too much to touch.

Something happens to two people who have been in a terrible fight; an intimacy develops. And all the more so if the fighters are not married, and are, on a day-to-day basis, not even close. A married fight, even an unusually brutal one, eventually fades back into the background of all the other hurts, but a fight with a colleague, it is like finding a brilliant ruby gem in a desert. It sits there, bright against the beige background. It becomes a point of almost purity. We will likely never speak of it again, this brief visibility.

But its effects, those remain obvious, at least to me, and to her as well. We are co-owners, after all, of this gem. "For my birthday," I said one day soon after Elisabeth took out her IFB. "For my birthday I would like to have an all-Broadway show."

And Barbara gave that to me, happily. It made me happy. I know she knows we have something there between us, sisters, mothers, daughters. The betrayal is the gem. How odd. It hurts to hold such a thing.

⌒

Ruthie, my Kabbala instructor, scolded me recently. "You, Rosie," she said in that Yiddish accent she has. "You, Rosie, you say you don't care about being famous, you don't care about your trophies, you let your children paint them, you hate your money and your fame, oh really? You, Rosie, are not honest with yourself. You love your money and your fame. If you really hated it, or didn't care, you would stay on *The View*, you would keep your small spot, but here you go, driven for a bigger thing, bigger lights, you learned nothing."

Ouch. But Ruthie's right. In some ways, *The View* was too small for me. As an artist, I feel I have the right to strive for more, more freedom of expression, for sure, but of course there's an element of something else in that striving too. More money. More attention. One must fight against those impulses. One must learn when enough is enough.

The View allowed me many things. It allowed me a measure of freedom I didn't have before. It allowed me to be a mother to my children. It allowed me sick days if I needed them. It allowed me a four-day workweek, school pickups, some time to paint. It allowed me a few vacations a year, but most important, it was, for better or worse, a team. I was not my own show. I was sharing the camera with three other women, and that can be less lonely, and sometimes more fun.

Part of growing up, of growing old, is learning when to give up the wheel. At some point, you need to realize you shouldn't even approach that intersection on your own. I don't think I'm near that point yet; my timing's still good, my hearing excellent. But it never hurts to practice. And if a part of that practice means lending Barbara an arm to lean on as she makes room in the driver's seat, helping her see she can't always see as well as she once could, and shouldn't be forced to anyway, then that might even be a small honor.

And yet, for all *The View* gave me, it also took its toll. In the end, it helped me to see that I need to find my own space, in cyberspace perhaps, a place where I can carve my own segments, where words are free, even if their repercussions aren't.

What I've learned from being a part of a corporation like ABC, is that you can't be really free. You need to edit what you say on air because the corporation cares; they have sponsors; they have advertisers. The corporation shapes your corps, your body, and the danger is that you'll eventually become a corpse. What I want for myself in the future is both connection and singularity, and it is this paradox, or contradiction, that may form the core of who I am, and fuel my work even as it confuses me. I'd like to be part of a team, yes, I would. But I'd also like to be radically alone, setting the standards, in charge and charging, defining and describing my own space, setting every rule and then breaking every rule I set, until I get tired. Until I get lonely. And then I want to go home. And then I want something simpler. Until I feel stifled by the sweetness and the strictures, and then I want my air back. It is hard, wanting your cake and eating it too. You can get fat that way. But, wow, the dreams you dream, the concoctions you cook, the breadth and depth of the banquet. I have been blessed.

When I was a child, my mother loved the two *Bs:* Barbra and Broadway. We played Streisand on the phonograph and heard her voice swell in our small suburban home. My mother died, and someday so will I. But I have her in my memory, and in the way I live my life, the things I love, and long for. Sometimes, when I go to see a Broadway show, I imagine my mother sitting next to me; she would be old now, in her seventies, but age doesn't dull the thrill you feel when the curtain opens and the chorus begins. Broadway is a street that goes on and on, a kind of infinity, the show that never stops. And that is why my mother loved it, and why I do too.

The season has ended and I think the hardest part is over. Just the other day, Barbara asked me if Kel and I would like to see the newest Broadway show in town, all three of us, together. The truth is, Kel and I had already seen the show, but what did that matter? There was something shy, and soft, in the way Barbara asked me. Might I turn her down? Might I say no? Might I stand up, scare her, walk away?

From *The View* I will walk away; but from Barbara, I know I won't. Out of this year many things have emerged, and most of them in five years will be utterly inconsequential, celebrity gossip, perhaps even forgotten. But one thing I think will remain the same, will remain solid, and that is the fact of a friendship formed, a tentative, testy, fretful friendship forged in both betrayal and a common core of hurt. My producer, Janette, told me that Barbara held my hand on the first day of *The View*'s new premiere last September—it seems so long ago— held my hand as we walked out onto the stage, and the audience cheered, hello, America.

Very little is for sure. The curtain's closing now. We're headed home. Picture this, if you can. The camera clicks. I am holding her hand as we go.

❧

Blog 6/21/07

endings

i dont read ur stupid blog
u r insulting me
what will people think
goodbye is never easy

a senior in highschool
its sunny and i wanna stay home
be done
move on

remember the drama
yearbook signing
with bubble letters
and perfect hearts

dont ever change
i will miss u in homeroom

have a good summer
keep in touch

most people dont
its how life works
in the moment only
fully alive

amy winehouse inspires me
get her cd
music is essential
defining decades

eltons daniel
came out the summer my mom died
stoney silence
in the station wagon

five fingers
in a hand
aunt minnies ring
a family
a fist

gotta kill the questions
for a while
the end is always rocky
one must focus

2 nite
kels 40th
loved ones arrived and ready
to celebrate all she is

weenie n jackie
so laughter is assured
cheers
all

All of Rosie's net profits from this book are being donated to Rosie's Broadway Kids charity (http://www.rosiesbroadwaykids.org). For more information on Rosie O'Donnell and her charities, go to rosie.com.